Fulfilling Your Destiny

FULFILLING YOUR DESTINY

E.C. Nakeli

Publishing today for tomorrow's generation

© 2012 by E.C. Nakeli

Published by Perez Publishing LLC – *www.perezpublishing.com* –

For your questions and publishing needs write to:
Perez Publishing
548 Congressional Drive
Westminster, MD, 21158
USA
Email: *perezpublishing@gmail.com*

Printed in the United States of America

All rights reserved. No part of this publication may be reproduced, stored in a retrieval system, or transmitted in any form or by any means—for example, electronic, photocopy, recording—without the prior written permission of the publisher. The only exception is brief quotations in printed reviews.

E. C. Nakeli

To contact the author, write to:
E.C. Nakeli
Perez Publishing
548 Congressional Drive
Westminster, MD 21158
USA
Email: *ecnakeli@yahoo.com*

Fulfilling Your Destiny / E. C. Nakeli

ISBN: 978-0-9850668-1-9

Unless underwise indicated, Scripture references are from THE HOLY BIBLE, NEW INTERNATIONAL VERSION®, NIV® Copyright © 1973, 1978, 1984, 2011 by Biblica, Inc.™ Used by permission. All rights reserved worldwide.

Cover Image: © Zach ESSAMA used by permission.

Cover/Interior Design: Zach ESSAMA - *graphicspartner@gmail.com*

Content

Dedication xiii
Foreword.. xv
Acknowledgements xix
Preface xxi
Introduction. 23
    You Were Predestined 25
    Visionlessness 31

Chapter One
A Life without Vision.. 31
    Making a Difference 35

Chapter Two
The Believer's Calling... 41
    1.   Called into Fellowship 42
    I   With the Father 42
    II   With the Son..43
    III With the Spirit 45
    Prayer 45
    Bible Reading 45
    Bible Meditation 46

	Worship	46
IV	With the Saints	46
2.	Called to Obedience	47
3.	Called to Live a Holy Life	48
4.	Called to Endure Suffering	50
5.	Called to Freedom	54
I	Freedom to Ask	55
II	Freedom to Approach	56
III	Freedom to Choose	57
6.	Called to a Hope	59
I	Hope beyond this Life	59
II	Hope for a New Home	59
III	Hope to See Him	60
	Our Hope Has a Responsibility	60
7.	Called to Eternal Life	61
8.	Called to Belong to Christ	64
9.	Called into God's Wonderful Light	66
10.	Called to share in Christ Glory	66
11.	Called to Bless	67
12.	You Have Been Called to a Prize	68

Chapter Three
The Believer's Pursuit 73

1.	The Kingdom of God	74
2.	Righteousness	75
3.	Love	76
4.	Instruction	76
5.	Wisdom	77
6.	Peace	78

Chapter Four
The Believer's Duty 83
    To Fear the LORD 84
    I   What it is not 84
    II   What it is 85
    i.   Keep your Tongue from Evil 85
    ii.   Keep your Lips from Speaking Lies 86
    iii. Turn from Evil and Do Good 86
    iv. Seek Peace and Pursue it 86
    How to Receive the Fear of the Lord 86
    i.   It Starts by Receiving an Undivided Heart
        from the Lord 87
    ii.   Ask Him to Inspire you to Fear Him 87
    iii. Be Willing to Learn 87
    The Benefits of Fearing the Lord 88
    i.   The Fear of the Lord is a Fountain of Life 88
    ii.   The Fear of the Lord is a Fortress 88
    iii. The Fear of the Lord is Wisdom 88
    iv. The Fear of the Lord Brings Wealth 89
    v.   The Fear of the Lord Brings Blessings 90
    vi. The Fear of the Lord Adds Length to Life 90
    vii. The Fear of the Lord Brings Provision 90
    viii. The Fear of the Lord Brings Protection 91
    ix. The Fear of the Lord Brings Healing 91
    x.   The Fear of the Lord Draws God's Compassion 91
    xi. The Fear of the Lord is a Store
        of God's Goodness 92
    xii. The Fear of the Lord Earns God's Confidence 92
    xiii. God's Love for those who Fear Him is Great 93

xiv. God Fulfils the Desires of those who Fear Him.....93
xv. The Fear of the Lord Sets your Name
in God's Special Book of Record...........................93
xvi. God Delights in those who Fear Him...................94
To Walk in His Ways...94
Why you Must Walk in His Ways.............................95
To Love the Lord..96
Manifestations of the Love for God 97
  i. Obedience...97
  ii. Sacrifice...98
  iii. Love for your Brother......................................98
  iv. Feeding the Sheep and Lambs of Christ................99
  v. In not Loving the World.................................99
To Serve the Lord your God 99
  i. With all your Heart...99
  ii. With all your Soul..100
  iii. With Faithfulness..100
  iv. With Willingness of Mind.............................100
  v. In the Fear of the Lord..................................100
The Danger of Pride in Service 101
Elements of Pride 102
Beware of Fame and Power......................................103
  i. Trying to Render Service beyond
His Grace and Faith 103
  ii. Despising the God-ordained
Ministry of Others..104
  iii. Despising the Authority of the Priest..................104

Acceptable Service 105
Why God Must Do it and not you. 107
i.   Durability 107
ii. What God Does is Final 107
iii. God Does everything to Reveal His Glory 107
iv. God alone Knows the Best
     Time for Everything 108
To Observe the Lord's Commands 108

Chapter Five
Satan's Strategy to Destroy Vision 113
Disguise 114
Distraction (Disorientation) 119
Displacement (Disconnection) 122
Discouragement (Demoralization) 125
Dismay 127
Division 129
Destruction 132
Recognize your Enemy 137

Chapter Six
Your Counter Strategy 137
Renounce, Recollect and Realign 139
Reposition and Reconnect 140
Reliance and Renewal 143
Revival 148
Reclaim (Redeem) 153
Receive 154

Chapter Seven
The Pathway to Receiving a Vision 159
   1.   Desire 162
   Rebekah 163
   Pharaoh's Daughter 164
   Moses 165
   David 166
   2.   Decision 166
   I   Encounter a Reaction 167
   II   Lead to Revelation 167
   III   Demand Responsibility 168
   IV   Mean Taking a Risk 169
   V   Finally, Decision Can Meet Refusal 170
   3.   Determination 170
   I   Determination Implies a Cross 173
   II   Determination Requires Conviction 173
   III   Determination Requires Commitment 174
   IV   Determination Requires Courage 174
   V   Determination Implies Consecration 175
   4.   Desperation 176
   I   Separation 177
   II   Surrendering 178
   III   Supplication 178
   IV   Sacrifice 179
   V   Delight 181
   VI   Delight Implies Concentration 182
   VII Delight Implies Cherishing 182

Chapter Eight
How to Accomplish Your Vision **187**
  1. Count the Cost..188
  2. Consider (Evaluate) your Resources....................189
  3. Carve out a Plan 189
  4. Communicate your Vision. 190
  5. Cooperate with Others 193
  6. Celebrate your Co-workers 194
  Inspiration from David..194
  1. Acknowledging the Lord..................................195
  2. Serve the Lord with a Wholehearted Devotion ...195
  3. Serve the Lord with a Willing Mind 195
  4. Seek the Lord for Details 196
  5. Work Hard 196
  In His Presence..201

Chapter Nine
How to Accomplish your Vision-2 .... **201**
  At the Foot of the Cross.......................................204
  Your Purpose Determines a lot 207

Chapter Ten
Some Truths about a God-given Task....................... **213**
  God's Commitment to you....................................216
  More Facts about a God-given Task......................217

Dedication

I humbly dedicate this book to the Sovereign Lord and King, Jesus Christ; that through the work of the eternal and glorious Holy Spirit, He may use it to help thousands, nay millions, who are seeking to know their purpose, to find and fulfill their destiny.

Foreword

One of the interesting movements going on in the Christian conversation today is the quest for meaning in being a Christian. The general proposition of the past that somehow being a Christian is the normal societal expectation or even that being a Christian is some automatic *"ticket to heaven"* is no longer meaningful. The questions being pursued in this book are more focused around what difference it makes in one's life to be a follower of Jesus.

To be a serious follower of Jesus is to understand that we have been transformed into a citizen of His kingdom here on earth. God has a mission and agenda for his kingdom that extends from generation to generation. He calls forth believers (disciples) from each generation to be his presence in the world at all times. This is both a corporate (church) presence as well as in individual calling and mission.

One of the highest callings of Pastors is to help their members to learn how to listen to God's voice and to follow those promptings. There are many voices and many needs that we can give to our life energy to pursue. However, the most important consideration for serious Christians is whether we have given ourselves to God's intended purpose. Too many church members either don't prayerfully seek God's vision or they are satisfied to just show up for worship on Sunday.

This book both stirs up the conviction to seek God's vision for our lives as well as practical teaching on how to discern and follow that vision. This would be an excellent tool for individual reading as well as small group study and discussion. Sometimes we need the counsel and insights of others in order to hear what God is saying to us.

Especially important is the ability to identify the tactics of the enemy intended to keep us from God's best in our lives. Oh how easily we can become distracted, drawn off focus, or encumbered with lesser tasks. It requires a clear sense of calling and direction in order to perceive the tactics of the enemy in our lives. It requires a deep passion of conscience and bold determination to reject our detractors and learn to turn away from those who would oppose or discourage us.

It is always amazing to ponder that God would choose to use carnal and finite people to carry out his eternal purposes in the world. He not only calls us into his purposes, he also equips us to accomplish our work. We are constantly enrolled in God's training program. One of the hardest lessons for most people to learn is that we don't accomplish God's vision with our own wisdom or superior effort. God brings down the mighty and lifts up the humble. In order to be mighty in our calling and purpose in life God first wants to form our character.

This is not a book about Christendom—how to raise up a larger or more effective church. For some folks, following God's vision for their life will mean special work, but for most folks this vision is more ordinary and backyard/home focused. One life vision is not more important to God than another. The importance to God, according to Scripture, is whether we are being faithful in the station he has placed us and whether we are using the gifts he has given us. Churches and serious disciples need tools to help discover those callings and gifts. The best work Pastors can do is design opportunities and methods for people to live into their God given vision for their life.

This book could be excellent required reading for discipleship training programs for churches large and small. Other effective models include individual discovery tools for persons to discern opportunities and personal gifts that they are equipped with, to bring into God's vision for them. Seasoned mentors are quite helpful for new or young believers as well. Story telling is a tool that many congregations ignore. One of the most powerful teachers is each other's stories.

God needs many ambassadors from generation to generation to bring his kingdom among men. The teachings and admonitions of this book are absolutely necessary in order to be faithful followers as God calls us to be.

Darrell Baer
Conference Minister for the Franklin Mennonite Conference of churches of Mennonite Church USA.

Acknowledgements

You know it's at times difficult to decide who to acknowledge as just almost everybody in your life makes a contribution in one way or the other.

Thank you so much, Emmanuel Zama for helping to type the manuscripts for no pay. You will be greatly rewarded. A big God bless you.

Thank you the Zama parents for allowing me use your PC and home for this work.

Thank you the Bekondos for your moral support, for understanding me when I stayed in the room alone for very long periods.

And you Dr. Fonjong, a big God bless you for your positive and encouraging comments.

To all my friends: Munzu, Kermit, Ricky, Moses, Alex and Dorine, Plunkert, Elizabeth Mbunya, Ruthie, Sally and those I'm not able to mention. Thank you for being there.

To my disciple maker, Brother Enoch Bisong, thank you.

To my mentors: Pastor Epamba Simon and mummy Grace Epamba, thank you for your love and favor.

To my mothers in the Lord: Mummy Philo, Mummy Ophelia, Mummy Martina, Aunty Claire, thank you all for your support.

To the youths and young adults of the CMFI Kumba assembly and the rest of the congregation, thank you for accepting my leadership and ministry.

Thank you Papa and Mama (Joseph and Comfort Bokwe) and the rest of the Nakeli family, for being a family indeed.

Thank you auntie Claire Asu for the first proofreading of the work. Thank you Ayi Mbile for your editorial skills, and thank you Zach Essama for your expertise in the interior design.

Many blessings to you all.

Finally and most importantly, Glory to the Eternal King of kings and Lord of lords who through the Eternal Spirit of Grace inspired me to write this book.

Preface

It was in 2005, seven years ago that the Lord inspired me to write this book. It was a delightful learning process for me as I sat to be taught by the greatest Teacher—God's Holy Spirit. As we wrote the words in these pages with Him I was humbled at what He was teaching me. What I learned and wrote then has been the guiding principles of my walk and work and I have seen these principles taken me from one level to another, ever closer towards His purposes for my life. I am sending this book out at this time with the hope and assurance that it will enable many to accomplish their vision and fulfill their God-ordained destiny. Though the message in this book was penned seven years ago, it is as relevant today and will be for the next generation to help bring people to fulfill their God-ordained purpose.

The fact that you have this book in your hand is a sign that you yearn to discover and accomplish His eternal purpose for your life. My sincere prayer for you is that the Lord will use these words to lunch and propel you to accomplish your purpose.

Introduction.

Every manufacturer makes a device for a purpose. There is a pre-conceived idea and intent, which his equipment after manufacture is designed to meet. Each automobile manufacturing company makes cars for a general purpose, transportation. But each car model is designed to transport a particular thing, with a particular capacity and to be driven in a particular kind of terrain. Even those cars designed for personnel transport are designed to provide different levels of comfort and safety. For effective productivity, car users must know the purpose-intent for each kind of car.

This is but a faint, very faint picture of the master manufacturer, God. According to His design, everything has been made on purpose; I call it destiny, in conformity with His Eternal will for the universe He created out of His own might, wisdom and love. And that purpose of His will surely come to pass even as He designed it. *"But the plans of God stand firm forever, the purposes of his heart through all generations."* (Psalm 33:10-11)

God has set His purpose for every nation and every man on this earth, but people and nations are trying to make plans for themselves which do not conform to God's own plan and purpose. Hence in His sovereignty, He foils and destroys the plans of the nations and purposes of the peoples.

Did you know that God designed even where each nation will be found on this planet? The Bible says,

> **26** From one man he made every nation of men, that they should inhabit the whole earth; and he determined the times set for them and the exact places where they should live. **27** God did this so that men would seek him and perhaps reach out for him and find him, though he is not far from each one of us. **28** "For in him we live and move and have our being". As some of your own poets have said, "We are his offspring".
> (Acts 17:26-28)

He determined the time and location where each individual will be. Why? So that men will seek Him and reach out for Him and find Him. I love verse 28. It says in Him we live and move and have our being.

- In Him we are really living
- In Him we move into our destiny.
- In Him we are what He set for us to be.

His plans stand firm forever!
His purpose through all generations!

Why? Because, like it is written elsewhere in His Eternal word, "He is mighty and firm in His purpose".

You Were Predestined

> In him we were also chosen, having been predestined according to the plan of him who works out everything in conformity with the purpose of his will.
>
> (Ephesians 1:11).

God determined the cause and outcome of each life in this universe. Each one, nay everything was predestined according to the plan of God. This plan is in conformity with His purpose. Throughout scripture, we see God reiterating the fact that His purpose will stand.

> "For I know the plans I have for you," declares the LORD, "plans to prosper you and not to harm you, plans to give you hope and a future."
>
> (Jeremiah 29:11)

God has a plan for you and only He knows the plan, but He gives you an overview of it; plans of prosperity, plans of hope, so as to bring you into your planned (predestined) future. The KJV puts it this way *"to give you an expected end"*. There is an end God has planned for you, and only He can lead you into that end. Life was not meant to be lived by chance, trying this and that, yet that's what so many people are doing. Some think because it worked for x, it's going to work for me and hence the many defeats and failures. Even if you try things out and they work if that was not God's purpose for your life you'll realize there is no satisfaction or sense of accomplishment within. Have you seen people with four PhD's? Have you ever asked yourself why on earth will someone dedicate so much time and energy for what will not be useful? The only reason is because such do not yet know their purpose and so life is lived on the basis of the opportunities which come along.

It does not matter who you are, where you were born, and the parents who gave birth to you nor your family background. God has a purpose for your life. His word says *"God is mighty and does not despise men; He is mighty, and firm in His purpose"* (Job 36:5).

> My frame was not hidden from you when I was made in the secret place. When I was woven together in the depths of the earth, your eyes saw my unformed body. All the days ordained for me were written in your book before one of them came to be.
> (Psalm 139:15-16)

Even your very buildup, the shape of your nose, ears, mouth, eyes, hands etc, all that is inside of you was designed according to God's purpose for your life. All your days have been ordained and written in a blueprint, which only God has. He has determined all of your life. So the solution to life is not trying out things here and there but to seek from Him that which He has in store for you.

God's number one plan for you is salvation. As you accept His plan of salvation, this brings you into a position where He can now lead you into His predetermined purpose for your life. Salvation in Christ Jesus is the only set way of getting on board

God's caravan leading you to your destiny. To reject God's plan of salvation is to reject His purpose for your life.

As you accept His salvation through Christ Jesus He gives you His Spirit who becomes your Counselor and Guide into His eternal plan and purpose for you. He will reveal to you step by step God's blueprint for your life as you trust and follow.

The Lord said to pharaoh:

> I have raised you up for this very purpose, that I might show you my power and that my name might be proclaimed in all the earth.
>
> (Exodus 9:16)

Thus, He purposed pharaoh to be raised for the demonstration of His power, that His fame and His Name might be proclaimed in all the earth.

To Jeremiah, he said:

> before I formed you in the womb I knew you, before you were born, I set you apart; I appointed you as a prophet to the nations.
>
> (Jeremiah 1:5)

God has appointed you to do something specific to influence this world God-ward. Seek to fulfill that purpose.

Of the Lord Jesus Christ it is said,

> This man was handed over to you by God's set purpose and foreknowledge; and you, with the help of wicked men, put him to death by nailing him to the cross.
>
> (Acts 2:23)

It's time for you to enter the destiny wagon, and in that wagon to your destiny you are the only passenger. Not even your wife or children or father or mother has a ticket into that wagon. For it has been written by the door according to the design of the manufacture, God the Father, *"driver and one person."* The driver of the wagon is the Holy Spirit though He may seem not to be there. You can trust Him to drive you safely through the bumps and potholes to destiny land. Do not attempt to help in the control, do not hold the steering wheel even if you think the driver is *"dozing off"*, but feel free to scream when your heart just beats a little faster. He understands.

This book is designed to get you on board your destiny wagon to destiny land and my prayer is that by the time you come to the end of it you'll just be there on board.

A FIVE-MINUTE STOP

✣ **Points to Meditate on:**

a. *Life was not meant to be lived by chance but by following God's original plan and purpose.*

b. *Salvation in Christ Jesus is the only set way of getting on board God's caravan leading you to your destiny.*

✣ **Decisions**

....
....
....
....
....
....
....
....
....
....
....
....
....

✣ Heartcry

"Father, it is true that you never meant for me to live my life trying things out; You designed me on purpose and only You have the blueprint of my design. Help me Lord, as I have accepted Your salvation, to follow You faithfully into my destiny."

A LIFE WITHOUT VISION

Visionlessness

3 When Adam had lived 130 years, he had a son in his own likeness, in his own image; and he named him Seth. After Seth was born, *4*Adam lived 800 years and had other sons and daughters. *5*Altogether, Adam lived 930 years, and then he died. *6*When Seth had lived 105 years, he became the father of Enosh. *7* And after he became the father of Enosh, Seth lived 807 years and had other sons and daughters. *8* Altogether Seth lived 912 years, and then he died […] *25* When Methuselah had lived 187 years, he became the father of Lamech and *26*had other sons and daughters. *27*Altogether Methuselah lived 969 years, and then he died. *28* When Lamech had lived 182 years, he had a son. *29* He named him Noah and said "he will comfort us in the labour and painful toil of

our hands caused by the ground the Lord has cursed." *30* After Noah was born, *31* Lamech lived 595 years and had other sons and daughters. Altogether, Lamech lived 777 years, and then he died.
(Genesis 5:3-8, 25-31)

10 This is the account of Shem.
Two years after the flood, when Shem was 100 years old, he became the father of Arphaxad. *11*And after he became the father of Arphaxad, Shem lived 500 years and had other sons and daughters.
*12*When Arphaxad had lived 35 years, he became the father of Shelah. *13* And after he became the father of Shelah, Arphaxad lived 403 years and had other sons and daughters. [...]
24 When Nahor had lived 29 years, he became the father of Terah. *25* And after he became the father of Terah, Nahor lived 119 years and had other sons and daughters.
26 After Terah had lived 70 years, he became the father of Abram, Nahor and Haran.
(Genesis 11:10-26)

27 This is the account of Terah.
Terah became the father of Abram, Nahor and Haran. And Haran became the father of Lot. *28* While his father Terah was still alive, Haran died in Ur of the Chaldeans, in the land of his birth. *29* Abram and Nahor both married. The name of Abram's wife was Sarai, and the name of Nahor's wife was Milcah; she was the daughter of Haran, the father of both Milcah and Iscah. *30* Now Sarai was barren; she had no children.
31 Terah took his son Abram, his grandson Lot son of Haran, and his daughter-in-law Sarai, the wife of his

son Abram, and together they set out from Ur of the Chaldeans to go to Canaan. But when they came to Haran, they settled there.
32 Terah lived 205 years, and he died in Haran.
(Genesis 11:27-32)

We live in a generation where many people irrespective of race, color, age, social status seem to live without any vision – no overriding purpose and drive in life. Many live with no intent of influencing the world, worse still, not leaving behind a legacy that will count even in the life beyond this. To a large category it is nothing but a belief of *"Let us eat and drink, for tomorrow we die"*.

I want you to take a careful look at the passages above. There seems to have been a pattern of purposeless living, generation after generation.

A life without vision is drudgery. It soon loses its taste and ends up in useless adventures. When there's no vision there's nothing to be realized or accomplished. A pattern of birth and death can be seen in the above passages, for the most part of it.

In the bracket of birth and death, God intended us to realize something bigger than us, beyond our natural abilities.

Now, vision is that thing bigger than you, which must be realized within the birth and death bracket with an influence beyond puny self.

Many people think all that is needed in life is passion. Passion for music, passion for sports, passion for this and that, but passion without purpose is more than useless. The only benefit of passion is to help us accomplish a greater objective.

When this objective isn't there, nothing but a wreck should be expected out of passion.

Passion without vision can make you a perpetual spectator who can risk it all for nothing.

Can you imagine how many lives have been lost because people have passion for things without purpose?

Visionlessness is the greatest disease that has plagued human kind since the fall.

For a moment I want you to ask yourself this question "If I should die today what will be written about me between birth and death?"

You say, *"my life history"*. Do you think the people mentioned in the passages above have no history? They certainly do have, just that it is not of sufficient worth to be recorded. They certainly worked to earn a living but there's nothing worth recording, to be passed to other generations, about them.

A visionless life is one without inspiration and for countless generations it shall remain without inspiration. Are the only things that can be mentioned about your life birth and death?

My greatest worry with visionlessness is that it can become generational. Parents passing down to their progeny visionlessness. Take a look at the passages again and you'll realize what I am saying.

I trust someone is saying, *"Yeah, I am visionless, but how do I get a vision?"* How do I make a difference?

Making a Difference

From the passage above, Genesis 11:10-32, there's at least someone who wanted to make a difference. Terah decided to break free from this drudgery of a life without meaning. He decided to break loose from the circle of those without purpose as a result of a disaster, which befell him. What do we see in this?

Disasters and misfortunes can be necessary to break one free from patterns of mediocrity and visionlessness. The death of a son set Terah to think. Making a difference always starts with a separation, parting company with all that which is mediocre. Terah's vision was Canaan, that was his destination but again we read *"... But when they came to Haran, they settled there."* (Genesis 11:31) Like Terah, so many who have dared to be purposeful have ended on the way to their purpose for several reasons. Many have settled on the way to their destination – Haran. We shall talk about this later.

For the moment I wish to appreciate Terah, for the bold step towards being purposeful by moving away from a circle of mediocre. The fact that he failed is a totally different story.

The need for separation is so important that it was God's initial prescription to Abram.

> The LORD said to Abram, "leave your country, your people and your father's household and go to the land I will show you".
> (Genesis 12:1)

There must be a breaking free from ties with mediocrity and purposelessness for God to work with us and through us. There must be a breaking free from failures of the past. There must be a breaking free from traditions and customs and people who can hinder one's purpose:

1. Those who have no vision and do not bother to have any. These are people whose lives are committed to nothing, whose only reason for living is because they were born and whose only goal is to continue a lineage. For such can never be an inspiration to you.
2. Those who failed and gave up; These are people who once had a vision and were committed to it but later gave it up for any and every reason. Such will see it impossible to accomplish any vision. I do not mean those who failed but are making use of their failures to continue their pursuit. Such are great resources.
3. The customs and believes and traditions and ways of those who have no purpose.
4. The customs, believes, traditions, ways and mindsets of those who failed and gave up.
5. The things and people who can be of no consequence to a purposeful life.

Unless there're these necessary separations, there can be no way to see what God wants to show you.

This was exactly the case with Abram. Though he left his country and father's household, Abram did not separate from his people. The Bible says, *"So Abram left, as the LORD had told him; and Lot went with him."* (Genesis 12:4a)

From then on, Lot was a barrier to Abrams vision, and as such he couldn't see clearly what the Lord had to show him. Every tie, anything we cling to, from which we ought to separate will only act as a hindrance to our purpose.

Though Abram, was now in Canaan he could not receive further light because he had not fully obeyed the command to separate. Because God had a greater purpose for Abram, He brought about a circumstance, which caused him to be separated from Lot.

God will create circumstances to separate you from all that you're clinging to which is unnecessary to the accomplishment of your vision.

The LORD only gave Abram further light and method of accomplishment when his separation from Lot was effected.

> *8* So Abram said to Lot, "Lets not have any quarrelling between you and me or between your herdsmen and mine for we are brothers. *9* Is not the whole land before you? Let's part company. If you go to the left I'll go to the right; if you go to the right I'll go to the left' […] *14* The LORD said to Abram after Lot had parted from him, 'Lift up your eyes from where you are and look north and south east and west. *15* All the land that you see I'll give to you and your offspring forever. *16* I'll make your offspring like the dust of the earth that if anyone could count the dust then your offspring could be counted, *17* go, walk through the length and breadth of the land, for I am giving it to you."
> (Genesis 13: 8-9, 14-17).

The questions you must ask yourself in the light of God's presence are:

"What is it that is hindering me from having a vision?"

"What are the entanglements I must break to have a forward drive towards my purpose?"

I would like us to see how you can get a specific purpose in life but before we do that, let's make sure you understand the reason for which you were saved.

I will call it, "The believer's calling".

A TEN-MINUTES STOP

✣ **Points to Meditate on**

a. *A life without vision is drudgery. It soon loses its taste and ends up in useless adventures.*

b. *The only benefit of passion is to enable you accomplish a greater objective. Passion without purpose is more than useless.*

c. *Visionlessness is a disease, which can become generational.*

d. *Unless you separate from all that can hinder your vision, there can be no way to see what God wants to show you.*

e. *God will create circumstances to separate you from all that you are clinging to which is unnecessary for the accomplishment of your vision.*

✣ **Decisions**

....
....
....
....
....
....
....

✤ Heartcry

"Gracious Lord, I do not want my life to continue to be drudgery; without any overriding purpose. I do not want to transmit purposelessness to my progeny. I do not want to have passion without purpose. Enable me to carry out the necessary separations so that I can receive from you my purpose for living."

THE BELIEVER'S CALLING

God has called every believer and we must labor to fulfill our calling. It is for this reason Peter said

> Therefore, my brothers, be all the more eager to make your calling and election sure.
> (2 Peter 1:10)

In order words, we must see to it that we accomplish our God-ordained purpose.

> **29** For those God foreknew He also predestined to be conformed to the likeness of His Son, that He might be the firstborn among many brothers. **30** And those He predestined, He also called; those He called, He also justified; those He justified, He also glorified.
> (Romans 8:29-30)

Why did God call you?

What did God call you for?

We shall seek to answer these questions in this chapter.

1. Called into Fellowship

To have fellowship with someone means the following:

- It means to be sharers and partakers.
- It means to have a common interest.
- It means companionship.

Now the Bible tells us we have been called into fellowship

I   With the Father

"We proclaim to you what we have seen and heard, so that you also may have fellowship with us. And our fellowship is with the Father and with His Son, Jesus Christ."
(1 John 1:3)

This means one aspect of the purpose of your life is to share in and be a partaker in the Father's eternal plan for mankind and the whole creation. It is sharing in His supreme will for the universe by being actively involved in the establishment of His will here "on earth as it is in Heaven". It is a call to share in the interests of the Father, the plans of the Father to bring everything under the rule of His One and Only begotten.

II With the Son

> We proclaim to you what we have seen and heard, so that you also may have fellowship with us. And our fellowship is with the Father and with his Son, Jesus Christ.
>
> (1 John 1:3)

> God who has called you into fellowship with His Son is faithful.
>
> (1 Corinthians 1:9)

The Father did not just call you and I into fellowship with Himself but also into fellowship with the Son. We are to share in His burdens for a lost world, in the interests of His death on the Cross, in the victory of His resurrection. This means being partakers in the accomplishment of the purpose for which the Father anointed Him:

- Preaching the Good News to the poor:

Who are the poor?

Those without any knowledge of God, yeah, the very poor in spirit.

- Proclaiming freedom for the prisoners:

Who are the prisoners?

Those locked in Satan's chains of deception, addiction, sin etc. We must proclaim freedom to such if we must share in His interests.

- Proclaiming recovery of sight for the blind.

Who are the blind?

Those whose minds the ruler of this age has blinded so they cannot see the light of the gospel of Christ Jesus.

- Releasing the oppressed:

Fellowship with the Son will mean releasing those under the oppression of sin, sickness, demons and fear of death. We need to see that men are set free or better still enter into their Christ-bought, God-given freedom.

- Proclaiming the year of the Lord's favor:

Is there any greater favor than the fact that God should cancel our debts through the death of His Son? Is there any greater favor than that this is the time of God's restoring to us, through the Cross, all that was stolen by the devil? (See Luke 4:18-19)

Fellowship with the Son will mean us working to see His Kingdom come.

Someone may object, that the fulfillment of this prophecy was for the Lord only. But I tell you; it is for you and I too. Was it not the same task He gave to Paul when He revealed Himself to him on the Damascus road and said:

> *17* I will rescue you from your own people and from the Gentiles. I am sending you to them *18* to open their eyes and turn them from darkness to light, and from the power of Satan to God, so that they may receive forgiveness of sins and a place among those who are sanctified by faith in me.
>
> (Acts 26:17-18)

III With the Spirit

May the grace of the Lord Jesus Christ, and the love of God, and the fellowship of the Holy Spirit be with you all.
(2 Corinthians 13:14)

You were called into fellowship with the Spirit. To make Him your companion! The very purpose for sending the Spirit is that He will make known to you and I, the will of the Father, teaching and reminding us of every command. (see John 14:26)

This can only be realized as we make Him our companion by identifying ourselves with His leadership.

What therefore are the avenues for fellowship with the Godhead?

Prayer

As we pray, we align ourselves with God's purpose for our lives, the church and the world. We give God the opportunity to work in us and through us as we pray, making us to conform to His character.

Bible Reading

As we read and study the word we get to know Him better, understanding His principles and ways as applied to us. As we read the word we create a spiritual well in us from which we can always draw for growth.

Bible Meditation

Bible meditation is deeper than just Bible reading or study. In Bible meditation we spend time with a particular verse or verses and allow the Spirit to give us light and understanding, most often as the verse applies to us at the moment or as He discerns for our future application.

Worship

Worship is the greatest avenue for fellowship with the Godhead; offering of our lives as *"living sacrifices, holy and acceptable"* to God. Bowing down to Him in humble adoration and reverence!

It is as we exploit these avenues of fellowship with the Godhead that we become spiritually empowered, cleansed and transformed characterwise to live victorious lives over sin, the world and the devil. Fellowship with the Father enables us to break every link of fellowship with the world. Fellowship with the Son enables us to break any tie of fellowship with the devil, and fellowship with the Spirit enables us to break every tie with sin and the flesh.

IV With the Saints

> We proclaim to you what we have seen and heard, so that you also may have fellowship with us. And our fellowship is with the Father and with His Son, Jesus Christ.
> (1 John 1:3)

The purpose of fellowship with the saints is for mutual encouragement and edification. Coming together and praying, sharing, worshipping etc. (1 Corinthians 14:26) goes a long way to help each other continue in the race and fulfill our God-ordained destinies.

2. Called to Obedience

> Through Him and for His name sake, we received grace and apostleship to call people from among all the Gentiles to the obedience that comes from faith.
> (Romans 1:5)

We have been called to live a life that stems from obedience, not by what we see and analyze but an obedience, which comes from faith.

What therefore is faith?

> Now faith is being sure of what we hope for and certain of what we do not see.
> (Hebrews 11:1)

To be sure and certain would mean

- Not liable to change or failure;
- Firm and unyielding;
- Stable;
- Free from doubt;
- Positive;
- Absolutely confident.

The whole passage of Hebrews 11 is that of people who obeyed God by faith, not by what was seen. We have been called to live a life of faith because to obey God, we need faith.

"We live by faith and not by sight" (2 Corinthians 5:7)

Why? *"Because without faith it is impossible to please God"* (Hebrews 11:6a), therefore *"we make it our goal to please Him"* (2 Corinthians 5:9a) in other words we make it our purpose to please God i.e. to obey Him by faith.

3. Called to Live a Holy Life

> For God did not call us to be impure but to live a holy life.
> (1 Thessalonicians 4:7)

> To the church of God in Corinth, to those sanctified in Christ Jesus and called to be holy, together with all those everywhere who call on the name of our Lord Jesus Christ – their Lord and ours.
> (1 Corinthians 1:2)

> Who has saved us and called us to a holy life – not because of anything we have done but because of His own purpose and grace.
> (2 Timothy 1:9a)

Permit me make a point very clear, before we proceed. We have been called to be holy and not to become holy. At conversion, Christ washed us and purified us from all sin and made us holy by clothing us in His own righteousness.

> And that is what some of you were. But you were washed, you were sanctified, you were justified in the name of the Lord Jesus Christ and by the Spirit of our God.
> (1 Corinthians 6:11)

- You were washed
- You were sanctified

- You were justified.

Thus our calling here is to, through the leadership of the Holy Spirit, maintain or keep ourselves from being polluted or contaminated. In other words we are to preserve our holiness by the power of the Spirit. That is why James could say

> Religion that God our Father accepts as pure and faultless is this; to look after orphans and widows in their distress and to keep oneself from being polluted by the world.
> (James 1:27)

It is thus the responsibility of the believer to be watchful and keep himself from pollution. Now we can only pollute what is pure and clean. If our task is to attain holiness we can't talk of *"Keeping oneself from being polluted by the world"*. How do we keep ourselves pure?

> It is God's will that you should be sanctified; that you should avoid sexual immorality; that each of you should learn to control his own body in a way that is holy and acceptable.
> (1 Thessalonicians 4:3-4)

- Avoiding sexual immorality
- Exercising self-control
- Breaking all fellowship with evil
- Breaking all friendship with the world
- Thinking about things which are pure

But in case you've allowed yourself to be contaminated, is all hope gone? Certainly not!

Since we have these promises, dear friends, let us purify ourselves from everything that contaminates body and spirit, Perfecting holiness out of reverence for God.
(2 Corinthians 7:1)

There's the blood available for cleansing through true repentance and forsaking of sin. This is how we perfect holiness, through a reverence for God. Reverence will keep us from any known and deliberate sin and from circumstances which can get us into sinning against God. It causes us to shun the very appearance of evil.

The question is *"are you living a holy life?"* Do you know a hatred for sin in your life?

Does the verse *"make every effort to live in peace and be holy; without holiness no one will see the Lord"* (Hebrews 12:14) make any sense or meaning to you?

Holiness is the work of the Spirit of God; yours is to actively submit to His leadership and working in your life.

4. Called to Endure Suffering

19 For it is commendable if a man bears up under the pain of unjust suffering because he is conscious of God. *20* But how is it to your credit if you receive a beating for doing wrong and endure it? But if you suffer for doing good and you endure it, this is commendable before God. *21* To this you were called, because Christ suffered for you, leaving you an example that you should follow in His steps.
(1 Peter 2:19-21)

The Believer's Calling

> For it has been granted to you on behalf of Christ not only to believe in Him, but also to suffer for Him.
> (Philippians 1:29)

This is rather *"unbelievable"* to many believers, especially the present-day ones who receive teaching upon teaching that Christians must be free from all forms of pain and suffering. And because of this we find the great compromises in the church today. Why? Because people will rather compromise than suffer pain. *"Christians"* would rather adopt the ways and principles of the world some very anti-gospel, than suffer persecution.

As believers, our calling is to hold up to the standards of our Lord and Savior Jesus Christ without fear of consequence.

Suffering is the very essence of discipleship if we are to follow in His footsteps.

If we are to hold to the standards, suffering is inevitable. We are not to bring the suffering upon ourselves but must be ready to endure it for the sake of the gospel as we give ourselves to preaching it and above all living it out.

Why must we endure suffering?

Because Christ suffered, leaving us an example to follow, and since no servant is greater than the master, we just must walk in His footsteps. The Bible says,

> **8** Although He was a son, He learnt obedience from what He suffered **9** and, once made perfect, He became the source of eternal salvation for all who obey Him.
> (Hebrews 5:8-9)

We suffer to learn obedience and to be made perfect. We suffer in order to become *"worthy"* of the glory we will share in the everlasting Kingdom of the Eternal King, Invincible, Immortal, and only wise.

> Now if we are children then we are heirs – heirs of God and co-heirs with Christ, if indeed we share in His sufferings in other that we may also share in His glory
> (Romans 8:17)

This indeed is what we may term fellowship in His suffering.

The Apostles suffered and endured it joyfully, counting it a privilege to suffer for that Name.

> The Apostles left the Sanhedrin, rejoicing because they had been counted worthy of suffering disgrace for the Name.
> (Acts 5:41)

What about those who have gone ahead of us?

> **36** Some faced jeers and flogging, while still others were chained and put in prison. **37** They were stoned; they were sawn in two; they were put to death by the sword. They went about in sheepskins and goatskins, destitute, persecuted and ill-treated – **38** the world was not worthy of them. They wandered in deserts and mountains, and in caves and holes in the ground.
> (Hebrews 11:36-38)

What about our Christian brothers in other lands? Do we think ours can be any different? May believers begin to break free from their comfort zones, yeah; worldly comfort to where even through suffering, can make an impact for Christ Jesus. For *"we must go through many hardships to enter the kingdom of God"* (Acts 14:22). This verse says we must; not we can or we may. In other words it must be part and parcel of our lives if we must enter the Kingdom.

Let us accept to be dismissed from work because we would not join the boss to cheat. Let us be maltreated because we would not have an affair with the boss. Let us be driven out of home, rejected by the very ones who claim to love us, just because we can't abandon the faith. Let us be mocked, we shall endure the shame. We prefer to stay with our low – pay jobs than work in a firm whose produce does not glorify the King. An attitude of enduring suffering is armor for the saint.

Suffering produces in us a people who are heaven bound as long as we are armed – with an attitude that accepts suffering for the sake of His Name.

> *1* Therefore, since Christ suffered in His body, arm yourselves also with the same attitude, because he who has suffered in his body is done with sin. *2* As a result, he does not live the rest of his earthly life for evil human desires, but rather for the will of God.
> (1 Peter 4:1-2)

Finally, "*12* Dear friends, do not be surprised at the painful trial you are suffering, as though something strange were happening to you. *13* But rejoice that you participate in the sufferings of Christ, so that you may be overjoyed when His glory is revealed. *14* If you are insulted because of the Name of Christ, you are blessed, for the Spirit of glory and of God rests on you. *15* If you suffer it should not be as a murderer or thief or any other kind of criminal, or even as a meddler. *16* However, if you suffer as a Christian, do not be ashamed, but praise God that you bear that Name. *17* For it is time for judgment to begin with the family of God; and if it begins with us, what will the outcome be for those who do not obey the gospel of God?"

(1 Peter 4:12-17).

5. Called to Freedom

It is for freedom that Christ has set us free. Stand firm, then, and do not let yourselves be burdened again by a yoke of slavery.

(Galatians 5:1)

You, my brothers, were called to be free. But do not use your freedom to indulge the sinful nature; rather, serve one another in love.

(Galatians 5:13)

The very plight of mankind today is bondage. Bondage to sin, bondage to wrong habits, bondage to sickness, bondage to demons, bondage to philosophies. In Christ Jesus, God has called us to be free from all these. It is part of realizing our calling when we enter into the fullness of our freedom. The greatest freedom a man can experience is the freedom from sin, for nothing enslaves and depraves a man like sin, no matter the form.

Ours is not just a freedom from but also a freedom to:

The Believer's Calling

I Freedom to Ask

12 I tell you the truth, anyone who has faith in Me will do what I have been doing. He will do even greater things than these, because I am going to the Father. *13* And I will do whatever you ask in My Name, so that the Son may bring glory to the Father. *14* You may ask Me for anything in My Name, and I will do it.
(John 14:12-14)

If you remain in Me and my words remain in you, ask whatever you wish, and it will be given you.
(John 15:7)

23 In that day you will no longer ask Me anything. I tell you the truth, My Father will give you whatever you ask in My Name. *24* Until now you have not asked for anything in My Name. Ask and you will receive, and your joy will be complete.
(John 16:23-24)

We have been given freedom to ask the Father for anything. *"Any"* means all without exception. The only preconditions are that

- We have faith in Him
- We remain in Him
- His words remain in us.

As we fulfill our call to fellowship and obedience, faith in Him and remaining in Him are just an outflow. For these make us become one with Him.

II Freedom to Approach

In Him and through faith in Him we may approach God with freedom and confidence.
(Ephesians 3:12)

Let us then approach the throne of grace with confidence, so that we may receive mercy and find grace to help us in our time of need.
(Hebrews 4:16)

We do not have just freedom to ask, but also freedom to approach. You know someone can give you freedom to ask but asking from afar, without getting into his immediate presence. Not so with the mighty King of kings and Lord of lords. The God of the universe has given us freedom to approach His Throne of Grace and make our needs and petitions known. We approach His Throne to receive mercy, we approach His Throne to find grace, all these to help us in our time of need. You know I've come to discover that God speaks, always, to His children from a point of mercy. All instructions He gives us come from a position of mercy.

He told Moses

> *21* And thou shalt put the mercy seat above upon the ark; and in the ark thou shalt put the testimony that I shall give thee. *22* And there I will meet with thee, and I will commune with thee from above the mercy seat, from between the two cherubims which are upon the ark of the testimony, of all things which I will give thee in commandment unto the children of Israel.
> (Exodus 25:21-22, KJV)

The commands of God are given us from His mercy seat, He communes with us i.e. speak and listens to us from His mercy seat. More and more let us exercise this freedom to approach, knowing that we are approaching His Throne of Grace. Is that not why John could say *"This is love for God: To obey His commands. And His commands are not burdensome"* (1 John 5:3)?

Burdensome means hard or heavy to bear, it means oppressive and crushing.

The KJV says, *"His commands are not grievous"*. When something is grievous it means it causes grief or sorrow, it means it is hurtful, destructive and injurious. God called us to freedom from all these.

III Freedom to Choose

"Everything is permissible for me" – but not everything is beneficial. "Everything is permissible for me" – but I will not be mastered by anything.
(1 Corinthians 6:12)

"Everything is permissible" – but not everything is beneficial. "Everything is permissible" – but not everything is constructive.
(1 Corinthians 10:23)

God has called us into freedom to choose, and He has given us His Spirit to lead us, and authorities to help us make right choices.

Nobody should seek his good, but the good of others
(1 Corinthians 10:24).

When the exercise of our freedom causes us to hurt others, it ceases to be Christlike freedom.

We should not use our freedom as license to sin or do wrong.

> But do not use your freedom to indulge
> the sinful nature
> (Galatians 5:13b).

The overall goal of our freedom of choice is to love and serve one another.

As you exercise your freedom, you should ask yourself, *"Am I serving others in love by the exercise of my freedom?"*

> So therefore "*13* Submit yourselves for the Lord's sake to every authority instituted among men: whether to the king, as the supreme authority, *14* or to governors, who are sent by him to punish those who do wrong and to commend those who do right. *15* For it is God's will that by doing good, you should silence the ignorant talk of foolish men. *16* Live as free men, but do not use your freedom as a cover up for evil; live as servants of God. *17* Show proper respect to everyone: love the brotherhood of believers, fear God, honor the king."
> (1 Peter 2:13-17)

The exercise of your freedom also means submission to authority and delegated authority. And in this you shall be fulfilling your calling.

6. Called to a Hope

There is one body and one Spirit – just as you were called to one hope when you were called.
(Ephesians 4:4)

I Hope beyond this Life

If only for this life we have hope in Christ, we are to be pitied more than all men.
(1 Corinthians 15:19)

We as Christians have a hope, which others cannot understand. We have a hope that spans eternity, hope beyond this life to a life in eternity, with God and His Christ. A life that is free from sorrow.

II Hope for a New Home

2 In my Father's house are many rooms; if it were not so, I would have told you. I am going there to prepare a place for you. *3* And if I go and prepare a place for you, I will come back and take you to be with me that you also may be where I am.
(John 14:2-3)

But in keeping with His promise we are looking forward to a new heaven and a new earth, the home of righteousness.
(2 Peter 3:13)

We have another home in view, a new home prepared by the Master Architect, the very One for whom, through whom and by whom this whole wide universe was made. Though they may drive us out of our earthly homes we shall endure it, for we have another home far greater than our earthly homes.

III Hope to See Him

> Dear friends, now we are children of God, and what we will be has not yet been made known. But we know that when He appears, we shall be like Him, for we shall see Him as He is.
> (1 John 3:2)

We have a hope to see the King, face to face, when He shall come in all His glory. We have a hope to become like Him at His appearance. O! How I long for that moment.

Our Hope Has a Responsibility

> Everyone who has this hope in Him purifies himself, just as He is pure.
> (1 John 3:3)

It is purification from all that contaminates.

> So then, dear friends, since you are looking forward to this, make every effort to be found spotless, blameless and at peace with Him.
> (2 Peter 3:14)

Thus as we fulfill our calling to a holy life, we are fulfilling the call to a hope. That's the responsibility of hope. It makes us responsible for the things we allow to get through the gates into our mind and spirit. Do you have hope to see Him? Then purify yourself from all that contaminates body, soul and spirit.

7. Called to Eternal Life

> Fight the good fight of faith. Take hold of the eternal life to which you were called when you made your good confession in the presence of many witnesses.
>
> (1 Timothy 6:12)

What is eternal life?

> Now this is eternal life: that they may know you, the only true God, and Jesus Christ, whom you have sent.
>
> (John 17:3).

Eternal life is knowledge of God and His Son. Not knowledge about God and His Son but of God and His Son. As we make it our goal to know God, He imparts to us His own very life so that even right now we begin to participate in the Divine nature of the Godhead.

There's something in scripture, which strikes me each time I come across it, it is the Lord's question to His disciples in Matthew 16.

> *13* When Jesus came to the region of Caesarea Philippi, he asked his disciples, "Who do people say the Son of Man is?" 14 They replied, "Some say John the Baptist; others say Elijah; and still others, Jeremiah or one of the prophets." *15* "But what about you?" he asked. "Who do you say I am?" *16* Simon Peter answered, "You are the Christ, the Son of the living God." *17* Jesus replied, "Blessed are you, Simon son of Jonah, for this was not revealed to you by man, but by my Father in heaven."
>
> (Matthew 16:13-17)

His first question was to know what His disciples had heard about Him. What is it they had learnt from others about His person? And for sure they all were quick to give a response. You can see the varying opinions of what others had of Jesus.

The Lord expects us to learn from others about Him but above all He wants us to know Him personally as revealed in His next question

"But what about you? Who do you say I am?"

This question was not to some strangers but to His own disciples who by this time had been with him for more than two years.

We can paraphrase the question in several ways:

- *"Though you have been around me for all this while, do you really know Me?"*
- *"Do you just depend on what others say about Me?"*
- *"What is it that you have discovered about Me?"*
- *"You've seen the miracles I've performed all these years, I've taught you for all this while; you've even cast out demons in My Name and performed miracles in My Name; your names are written in the Book of Life, but do you really know Me?"*

Knowledge of God and His Son can only be gotten through revelation, as the Father reveals the Son to us and as the Son reveals the Father to us.

Flesh and blood cannot reveal God to us but can only help us receive a revelation of God.

> I keep asking that the God of our Lord Jesus Christ, the glorious father, may give you the Spirit of wisdom and revelation, so that you may know Him better.
> (Ephesians 1:17)

We must ask God daily for revelation knowledge. Nothing pleases the Father like His children seeking to know Him and actually knowing Him.

> **23** This is what the Lord says:
> "Let not the wise man boast of his wisdom
> or the strong man boast of his strength
> or the rich man boast of his riches,
> **24** but let him who boasts boast about this:
> that he understands and knows me,
> that I am the Lord, who exercises kindness,
> justice and righteousness on earth,
> for in these I delight,"
> declares the Lord.
> (Jeremiah 9:23-24)

We live in a generation where there's a lot of boasting. People boast of their wisdom, wisdom that is earthly and of the devil (James 3:14-16). Others boast of their riches like the rich fool (Luke 12:21) not knowing God can demand of them their life at any time He wills. Still others boast of their power: political, financial, social, economic, material, and intellectual power.

God delights in you knowing Him as a God of kindness and compassion; One who seeks to meet your needs, forgive and restore you; One who longs to heal your wounds and teach you how to live an effective life.

He wants you to know Him as the God of justice, a God who does not show partiality; One who will judge every sin and rebellion. There's so much sin in the church today because believers have failed to know God as the God of justice, and thus the total lack of reverence for God; reverence which will bring about the total shunning of all sin.

Thirdly, He wants us to know Him as the God of righteousness, holy and pure; One who has no darkness in Him, One who will not tolerate sin in His presence. Such knowledge will produce in us a quest for holiness.

8. Called to Belong to Christ

> And you also are among those who are called to belong to Jesus Christ.
> (Romans 1:6)

To belong to means, to be part of, it means to be owned by someone.

Christ Jesus has called you into a total and irreversible ownership by Him. You were bought with His own very blood, such a costly price. To belong to Christ means to live for Him. This is the very essence of His death on that cruel tree.

> And He died for all, that those who live should no longer live for themselves but for Him who died for them and was raised again.
> (2 Corinthians 5:15)

He died that you may live for something other than you, something bigger than selfish accomplishments. He died that you may live for Him: His Name, His Kingdom, and His Glory.

> Do you not know that your bodies are members of Christ Himself?
>
> (1 Corinthians 6:15a)

> **19** Do you not know that your body is a temple of the Holy Spirit, who is in you, whom you have received from God? You are not your own; **20** you were bought at a price. Therefore honor God with your body.
>
> (1 Corinthians 6:19–20)

You have been called to honor God with your body. God is so jealous for you and I because He purchased us at such a tremendous cost. We grieve Him and make ourselves enemies of God each time we flirt with the world in its values, ways, standards, principles and methods.

Can you allow your spouse to commit adultery just once a week?

Can you allow your spouse to sleep with the enemy who is seeking your life just for a single night?

Yet, that's what happens when believers love the world or make friendship with this world (1 John 2:15; James 4:4). Your body is God's temple. Now the way you treat that body of yours depends on your attitude and mindset; do you see it as just your body or as God's temple?

There're things which may be *"good for the body"* but are however *"bad for God's temple"* and unless our attitude is that of totally belonging to Christ, of being the temple of the living God, we shall just crave for the wrong things.

9. Called into God's Wonderful Light

> But you are a chosen people, a royal priesthood, a holy nation, a people belonging to God, that you may declare the praises of Him who called you out of darkness into His wonderful light.
>
> (1 Peter 2:9)

As children of light you and I have been called to shine like stars and influence this depraved generation in godliness. The Lord said, "You are the light of the world" (Matthew 5:14). And that's what God has made of us, to show the way out of darkness into the light of God. You are to *"let your light shine before men, that they may see your good deeds and praise your Father in Heaven."* (Matthew 5:16).

Your acts of goodness and kindness are means to letting your light shine before men. You must walk in the light to keep your light shining.

> For you were once darkness, but now you are light in the Lord. Live as children of light.
>
> (Ephesians 5:8)

10. Called to Share in Christ Glory

> He called you to this through our gospel, that you might share in the glory of our Lord Jesus Christ.
>
> (2 Thessalonicians 2:14)

> And the God of all grace, who called you to His eternal glory in Christ, after you have suffered a little while, will Himself restore you and Make you strong, firm and steadfast.
>
> (Peter 5:10)

God has called you to be a sharer in the glory of His one and only Son, Jesus Christ. What is the glory of Christ: His power and authority. His sinlessness. His mandate to be always heard by the Father. His oneness with the Father in His will and interest. His self-effacement and triumph over sickness, sin and death—the glory of His resurrection.

Again you can only truly share in His glory as you allow the Holy Spirit to carry out His sanctifying work in your life.

11. Called to Bless

> Do not repay evil with evil or insult with insult, but with blessing, because to this you were called so that you may inherit a blessing.
>
> (1 Peter 3:9)

In a world so full of cursing and revenge, you have been called not just to be a blessing to the people around you but also to bless them. You have been called to actively bless those whom you encounter, no matter what they are. In blessing, you also will inherit a blessing. This is a spiritual principle on which you've been called to act. Bless them by your words; bless them with your love and gifts. Bless through all righteous means. Fulfill your calling to bless. Ask God daily for whom you must bless.

Last but not the least

12. You Have Been Called to a Prize

I press on towards the goal to win the prize for which God has called me heavenwards in Christ Jesus.
(Philippians 3:14)

We have now moved from the general to the specific. As individuals, God has called us to different prizes depending on the work He has for us. We can however not get to this stage unless we are fulfilling the general call as seen in the first eleven points. You have your own goal and prize for which you must work. It is your responsibility to seek the face of God in order to know that which He'll have you accomplish. This is what I term a vision. Others call it a goal or purpose and still others call it destiny. Whatever the appellation, the meaning remains the same.

Have you found out your vision?

A TWENTY-MINUTES STOP

✦ Points to Meditate on

a. *The call to fellowship is a call to share in the interests of the Father; His plan to bring everything under the rule of His One and Only Son.*

b. *It is as you exploit all the avenues for fellowship with the Godhead that you become spiritually empowered, cleansed and transformed characterwise to live a victorious life over sin, the world and the devil.*

c. *You are not complete in yourself. You need fellowship with other saints so as to be built up.*

d. *It is your responsibility to watch and keep yourself from pollution.*

e. *Suffering is the very essence of discipleship if you are to follow in His footsteps.*

f. *Nothing enslaves and depraves a man like sin, the greatest freedom anyone can experience is freedom from sin.*

g. *When the exercise of your freedom causes you to hurt others, it ceases to be Christlike freedom.*

h. *Hope makes you responsible for the things you allow to get into your mind and spirit.*

i. Though God expects you to learn about Him from others He passionately wants to reveal Himself to you personally.

j. God is jealous for you because He purchased you at such a tremendous cost.

✣ Decisions

✣ Heartcry

"Dear Father, You called me into fellowship with you, with Your dear Son, and with the blessed Holy Spirit. I want to exploit all these avenues for fellowship so as to be cleansed, empowered and transformed to live life victoriously. I want to live ever in the freedom You have given me, taking others into consideration. Help me Lord to fulfill my calling, knowing You purchased me at such a great cost.

Chapter Three

THE BELIEVER'S PURSUIT

A pursuit is that which a man is running after permanently. We live in a world in which people are continuously running after sex, fame, money, luxury and power. Should the believer run after such things? Certainly not!

> This is what the Lord says: what fault did your fathers find in me that they strayed so far from Me? They followed worthless idols and became worthless themselves.
> (Jeremiah 2:5)

Every body becomes like what he or she is pursuing. What is your pursuit? Money? Fame? Power? Material things and all else this vain world can offer?

In the sight of God all these things are worthless and all who run after them become as worthless. What is your worth in the eyes of God?

If the believer is not to pursue these things, what then should the one who desires, better still, yearns to fulfill his God-ordained destiny pursue? I tell you these in this section.

> But you, man of God, flee from all this, and pursue righteousness, godliness, faith, love, endurance and gentleness.
> (1 Timothy 6:11)

> Flee the evil desires of youth, and pursue righteousness, faith, love and peace, along with those who call on the Lord out of a pure heart.
> (2 Timothy 2:22)

These then are the things one who must fulfill his destiny should pursue:

1. The Kingdom of God

> But seek first his kingdom and his righteousness, and all these things will be given to you as well.
> (Matthew 6:33)

You are to pursue the Kingdom of God; the establishment of that Kingdom upon this earth, the reign of that Kingdom within you, the interest of that Kingdom, the glory of that Kingdom, the values of that Kingdom, the ways of the Kingdom and the power and the honor of the Kingdom. Yeah, you are to seek the King of that Kingdom-the eternal Lord and

Christ, Jesus the Son of God. Let His Kingdom reign within you and the power of the kingdom shall flow through you.

2. Righteousness

> But seek first his kingdom and his righteousness, and all these things will be given to you as well.
> (Matthew 6:33)

> He who pursues righteousness and love finds life, prosperity and honor.
> (Proverbs 21:21)

The believer is to pursue righteousness. To be clothed more and more with the righteousness of God. You must seek to do that which is right in the sight of God. That is righteousness; doing what is right before God. You may be where unrighteousness reigns all about. Noah was one such in his generation yet never gave up his pursuit of righteousness. Lot was another such pursuer of righteousness in his generation, which was soaked in sin and all kinds of unrighteous practices yet he kept his pursuit of righteousness.

People run after prosperity and honor. These people are trying to put the cart before the horse, no doubt all the shipwrecks. The Bible says, pursue righteousness, and you will find life, prosperity, and honor.

Do you want to be prosperous? I mean the kind of prosperity, which comes with life and honor. As you seek the righteousness of God, He adds all the things you need in life.

3. Love

> He who pursues righteousness and love finds life, prosperity and honor.
> (Proverbs 21:21)

Pursue love. Love for God and love for man. Love for the interest of His Kingdom. Seek and look for opportunities to show and practice love. It may mean you contributing to the need of that brother; material, financial or emotional. Look for opportunities to offer your service to the needy you meet around.

4. Instruction

> Hold on to instruction, do not let it go; guard it well, for it is your life.
> (Proverbs 4:3)

> Choose my instruction instead of silver, knowledge rather than choice gold.
> (Proverbs 8:10)

Instruction here talks of imparted knowledge. The Bible exhorts you to hold on to instruction and never let it go. Look for opportunities to receive knowledge, useful and profitable knowledge, which will help you, accomplish your vision. Seek the counsel of godly men and women who have gone ahead of you on this road you are now treading. Give yourself to study the word of God. By so doing, you are seeking instruction from Him. Labor to guard the knowledge or instruction you have received.

The LORD says, if offered silver or gold and also instruction, let go the silver and gold and pursue and acquire instruction. What does this mean practically? It means if making money will compete with an opportunity to learn from the Word, rather go and learn and acquire knowledge than the money-making routine. It means do not let go acquired knowledge even for the price of silver and gold.

5. Wisdom

> Turning your ear to wisdom and applying your heart to understanding.
> (Proverbs 2:2)

> For wisdom is more precious than rubies, and nothing you desire can compare with her.
> (Proverbs 8:11)

There's nothing like possessing godly wisdom. The Bible says, *"if any of you lack wisdom, he should ask God, who gives generously to all without finding fault; and it will be given to him."* (James 1:5). It is your responsibility to ask God for wisdom and hold on to Him to give it to you, *"for the LORD gives wisdom, and from His mouth come knowledge and understanding".* (Proverbs 2:6)

He who has wisdom possesses prudence, the virtue that will cause you to avoid unnecessary loss and injury.

He who has wisdom has knowledge – the clear and certain apprehension of truth.

He who has wisdom possesses discretion, the virtue that leads you to exercise cautious and correct judgment whether to do or not to do.

6. Peace

> Follow peace with all men, and holiness, without which no man shall see the Lord.
> (Hebrews 12:14 KJV)

The Bible exhorts you to run after peace and keep running after peace. Do everything to live at peace with all men as far as it is in your power to do so.

What do the above six pursuits sum up to? They sum up to running after the Lord Jesus Christ. Why? Because Christ Jesus *"has become for us wisdom from God that is, our righteousness, holiness and redemption."* (1 Corinthians 1:30) and *"He himself is our peace"* (Ephesians 2:14).

So you were redeemed to pursue and keep on pursuing, seek and keep on seeking the LORD. The LORD invites you to seek Him and to do so diligently. To seek God you need a God hunger and a God thirst, which will set you in motion and propel you along. The Lord says, *"you will seek Me and find Me when you seek Me with all your heart."* (Jeremiah 29:13)

David expressed his passion for God in the following words

> *1* As the dear pants for streams of water so my soul pants for you, O God. *2* My soul thirsts for God, for the living God. When can I go and meet with God?
> (Psalm 42:1-2)

When God sees such hunger and thirst for Him in your heart, He will reveal Himself in ways that will create more hunger and thirst for Him in your heart.

Finally you were created for His pleasure and so make it your goal to please Him.

> Thou art worthy, O Lord, to receive glory and honor and power: for thou hast created all things, and for thy pleasure they are and were created.
> (Revelation 4:11 KJV)

Yeah all things were made and exist for His pleasure. And so we seek always to offer ourselves as a living sacrifice; holy, pleasing and acceptable to God.

> And he died for all, that those who live should no longer live for themselves but for him who died for them and was raised again.
> (2 Corinthians 5:15)

If you lack hunger for God then this prayer is just for you.

> O Lord, I pray for mercy
> For my guilt, surely is plenty
> And my heart, void and empty
> Of love and compassion divine
> For those who have gone astray
> From the true and only Way.

Truly my heart is cold
Far from the Spirit's burning flame
Which makes feeble men bold
To stand in the Victor's Name
Like Your apostles of old
Despising all loss and shame.

Create in me a burning desire
Fueled by the Spirit's fervent fire
For souls streaming to hell's gate
To turn them from doom's fate
To Christ who gives hope and a future
And power over man's sinful nature.

Let me, from You borrow
A heart full of love and sorrow
For those who refuse to follow.
Let me walk the path Jesus trod
Saving men from the Judge's rod
Making them sons of the Most High God.

E.C. Nakeli
04/30/05

A FIVE MINUTES STOP

✤ **Points to Meditate on**

a. *Everybody becomes like what he or she is pursuing*
b. *Until God's Kingdom reigns within you His power cannot flow though you.*
c. *When God sees hunger and thirst for Him in your heart, He will reveal Himself to you in a way that will create more hunger and thirst for Him in your heart.*

✤ **Decisions**

✤ Heartcry

"Blessed Savior, I want to become like nothing else and like none else but You. I, therefore, make You my pursuit; the only thing worthy of my attention. I submit myself to the reign of Your Kingdom in me so that your power can flow through me. Create in me, O God, an ever increasing hunger and thirst for You."

THE BELIEVER'S DUTY

To fulfill your destiny you must fulfill your responsibility that is, your moral obligation to your creator – God. He revealed this obligation to Israel. In this dispensation of ours, He has made His infinite grace available to enable us, and His Spirit to lead us into doing His will i.e. keeping His laws. In the book of Ezekiel this is His promise

> *26* I will give you a new heart and put a new spirit in you; I will remove from you your heart of stone and give you a heart of flesh. *27* And I will put my Spirit in you and move you to follow my decrees and be careful to keep my laws.
>
> (Ezekiel 36:26-27)

His promise is for a new heart, a new spirit and also His Spirit. These are to enable us to:

1. Follow His decrees.
2. Be careful to keep His laws.

The duty of the believer is summarized in this passage.

> *12* And now, O Israel, what does the LORD your God ask of you but to fear the LORD your God, to walk in all his ways, to love him, to serve the LORD your God with all your heart and with all your soul, *13* and to observe the LORD's commands and decrees that I am giving you today for your own good?
> (Deuteronomy 10:12-13)

If you have never known your duty as a child of God, then know it now:

1. To fear the LORD
2. To walk in all His ways.
3. To love Him.
4. To serve the LORD your God.
5. To observe the LORD's commands and decrees.

To Fear the LORD

I What it is not

The fear of the Lord is not fright; it is not the tendency to look at God as One who is ready to strike each time you stumble, nor is it fear of punishment.

The Believer's Duty

II What it is

The fear of God is that deep respect which a believer has for God, His Name and His holiness.

The Bible in several passages tells us what the fear of God is. I cite some: *"To fear the Lord is to hate evil, ..."* (Proverbs 8:13)

Here the Bible defines the fear of the Lord as that capacity and tendency to hate evil. What is evil? Just anything that hasn't got its origin from the moral laws of the universe. Evil is anything, which cannot stand the presence of the Holy God, anything that is against His revealed will. The first manifestation of the fear of God is the capacity to hate sin.

> *11* Come, my children, listen to me;
> I will teach you the fear of the Lord.
> *12* Whoever of you loves life
> and desires to see many good days,
> *13* keep your tongue from evil
> and your lips from speaking lies.
> *14* Turn from evil and do good;
> seek peace and pursue it.
> (Psalm 34:11-14)

Here again we see the fear of the Lord as the capacity to

i. Keep your Tongue from Evil

This implies keeping your tongue from all that God does not like; gossip, slander, and cursing. Just anything which can hurt or wound the spirit of another.

ii. Keep your Lips from Speaking Lies

Lies telling is just as grievous to God as any other sin is. No matter the purpose or reason behind any lie, it remains a lie. The fear of God constraints the man who possesses it to speak the truth in spite of the constrains.

iii. Turn from Evil and Do Good

The fear of the Lord is that which constrains you to abandon what you may be involved in ignorantly and then realize it is wrong. No matter how much you may have invested in it, the fear of the Lord will cause you to abandon it and turn to the right direction.

iv. Seek Peace and Pursue it

It is the virtue which causes you to take the path of peace as far as it depends on you.

How to Receive the Fear of the Lord

The fear of the Lord is not natural. We are not born with it. It is God – given and so you can only receive it from the Lord. Now the question is *"How"*? The Lord promised:

> *39* I will give them singleness of heart and action, so that they will always fear me for their own good and the good of their children after them. *40* I will make an everlasting covenant with them: I will never stop doing good to them, and I will inspire them to fear me, so that they will never turn away from me.
>
> (Jeremiah 32: 39-40)

i. It Starts by Receiving an Undivided Heart from the Lord

This takes place at conversion when you repent from your sins and ask God for a new heart. Here the Lord talks of singleness of heart and action i.e. your actions tying with that which is in your heart. The psalmist cried out to God, *"give me an undivided heart that I may fear your Name"* (Psalm 86:11b). That's the starting point, asking God for an undivided heart.

ii. Ask Him to Inspire you to Fear Him

In the passage above in Jeremiah 32, He says He will inspire you to fear Him. Ask Him for that and be willing to be led into practicing what you ask for.

iii. Be Willing to Learn

The fear of the Lord grows in us as we learn through the trials and temptations we face daily.

> Remember the day you stood before the LORD your God at Horeb, when he said to me, "Assemble the people before me to hear my words so that they may learn to revere me as long as they live in the land and may teach them to their children."
> (Deuteronomy 4:10)

God's intention was also that the Israelites should learn to revere Him. So it was a virtue to be acquired through a learning process. Be willing to learn from mistakes; yours and others'.

The Benefits of Fearing the Lord

Every Christian virtue carries with it benefits. It is impossible to get the blessings without the virtue. How often do we try to claim blessings when we are not in possession of the virtues which put forth the blessings and failed woefully?

i. The Fear of the Lord is a Fountain of Life (Proverbs 14:27)

A fountain is simply the origin and source of something. He who fears the Lord has the very source of life in him, which he can give to others. The life in him bubbles like a fountain from which others can drink.

ii. The Fear of the Lord is a Fortress (Proverbs 14:26)

A fortress is simply a stronghold, a place of safety, a hiding place from an enemy during times of war. Ours is a life of continuous warfare. War against sin, war against the flesh, war against the world and the things of the world and war against the devil himself. The best place to live such a life is to be constantly in a fortress, and that fortress is the fear of the Lord. Nothing makes a man vulnerable to enemy attack like sin does. Sin is an open door to disease, sickness and demons. The fear of the Lord will keep you from sin and therefore from all these.

iii. The Fear of the Lord is Wisdom (Job 28:28, Psalm 111:10)

The wisdom mentioned here is godly wisdom, that which leads you to do things God's way. The Bible talks of two kinds of wisdom, worldly wisdom and godly wisdom. Such wisdom, which the fear of the Lord brings, is

- Pure
- Peace loving
- Considerate
- Submissive
- Full of mercy
- Impartial
- Sincere

These are the qualities of godly wisdom as described in James 3:13.

The fear of the Lord gives you wisdom, which will always be considerate and submissive to authority. If yours is wisdom which causes you to despise others and even authority then it certainly is not from God.

iv. The Fear of the Lord Brings Wealth (Proverbs 22:4)

We live in a world in which people think the only means to make wealth is by cheating others and gambling and all ungodly stuff. The word of God tells us that the fear of the Lord brings wealth and honor. Do you see that? Wealth and honor! There are people, many such, with wealth without honor. Such can go the whole way to behave like animals and gratify their animalistic passions and sensations for the sake of wealth. He who fears the Lord will be wealthy along with honor.

v. The Fear of the Lord Brings Blessings (Proverbs 28:14)

Psalm 128 lists the kind of blessings, which follow the one who fears the Lord:

- You will eat the fruit of your labor
- Blessings and prosperity will be yours
- Your spouse will be fruitful
- Your children will be fruitful.

What blessings!

vi. The Fear of the Lord Adds Length to Life (Proverbs 10:27)

What does this mean practically? It means he who fears the Lord has his days lengthened. Say if you were to live for 75 years because you fear the Lord you may now live for 80yrs. This is the word of God, do you believe it? The fear of the Lord causes you to live longer. After all is the fear of the Lord not the fountain of life? You wonder if this can really be true, what about the case of Hezekiah? He made his appeal to God on the basis of his fear of God and he had fifteen more years added to him.

vii. The Fear of the Lord Brings Provision (Psalm 34: 9-10)

God is committed to meet the needs of those who fear Him. The Bible says those who fear Him lack nothing. Let His Word be true and all else be false. Nothing means nothing. Every need met. All that you need, to live life one day at a time

God will give you. Though He may never satisfy your wants, he surely will meet your needs.

viii. The Fear of the Lord Brings Protection (Psalm 34:7)

Men travel over land and sea across nations and continents to seek protection from sources, which indeed can't offer them any true protection. For the child of God, the fear of the Lord brings you protection and deliverance from every danger. The Bible says "His angel encamps around those who fear Him"

ix. The Fear of the Lord Brings Healing (Malachi 4:2)

Apart from the fact that the fear of the Lord saves you from the coming wrath of God on all the unjust, arrogant and evil doers, He promises "the sun of righteousness with healing in it's wings", healing in every domain of your life.

x. The Fear of the Lord Draws God's Compassion (Psalm 103:13)

He told Moses,

> I will have mercy on whom I will have mercy and I will have compassion on whom I will have compassion.
> (Exodus 33:19).

It's all a matter of choice therefore on the part of the Lord and He says His choice is based on the fear of the Lord. He has decided to extend His compassion to all those who revere His Name. The fear of the Lord pushes us to treat God's things with respect and honor. It is what will move you to give Him the first place in your life, knowing that He is deserving of all that you are and have.

Throughout the scriptures you notice that whenever a king or the whole nation of Israel was living in some kind of disobedience and God promised judgment, or say a prophet confronted that individual with the word of the Lord, those who through respect and fear of the Lord repented received compassion but those who did not repent brought on themselves the promised judgment.

xi. The Fear of the Lord is a Store of God's Goodness (Psalm 31:19)

If you read the whole of Psalm 31 you can see the various ways in which God manifested His goodness to David.

- Deliverance, in verse one
- Protection, in verses 1 & 20
- Vindication, in verses 4 & 20
- Leadership, in verse 3
- Guidance, in verse 3
- God's favor, in verse 16

All these he said, God bestows in the sight of men.

xii. The Fear of the Lord Earns God's Confidence (Psalm 25:14)

Isn't it true that God has done nothing throughout history without confiding in one of His servants? When He wanted to destroy the world at the time, He confided in Noah. When He wanted to destroy Sodom and Gomorrah, He confided in Abraham and He has confided in His prophets throughout history. He reveals to those who fear Him the secrets of His Kingdom.

xiii. God's Love for those who Fear Him is Great (Psalm 103:11)

God is love and He loves all that He has made with an undying love. However His love for those who fear Him, the Bible says, is great. Greater than anyone can ever imagine *"as high as the heavens are above the earth"*. Can you tell me what that height is?

xiv. God Fulfils the Desires of those who Fear Him (Psalm 145:18-19)

The fear of the Lord leads us to a point where our desires become one with His. We begin to long for nothing but that which He wants of us and for us. A passion for His will for our lives is developed and we thus seek nothing but what pleases Him. At such a level, whatever we desire have its origin from Him and will find fulfillment in Him. Isn't it great to arrive at such a point in our walk with Him?

O God, bring me to that level of a total identification with You in Your desires and longings and interests.

xv. The Fear of the Lord Sets your Name in God's Special Book of Record (Malachi 3:14-16)

In a generation where the fear of the Lord, true reverential fear of the Lord is a rare virtue, where people consider it futile to serve God, where people see no need or blessing or gain in serving the Lord, forgetting that *"godliness with contentment is great gain"*.

Where the arrogant are considered blessed,

Where evildoers appear to be more prosperous,

Where those who challenge God seem to go unpunished,

God has decided to open a special record of those who fear Him and bring honor to His Name.

xvi. God Delights in those who Fear Him (Psalm 147:11)

To delight in something is to take and find pleasure and satisfaction in the thing. If God delights in those who fear Him then He certainly takes pleasure in them. Who wouldn't want his creator–God to take pleasure in him?

What list of benefits! And it can go on and on. As you fear the Lord you fulfill your God-ordained destiny even as you are brought into all these benefits, which come along with the fear of the Lord.

To Walk in His Ways

Your number two duty as a child of God, or just any one living in this universe of God's is to walk in the ways of the Lord. There are the ways of God and the ways of the world and the ways of man. The ways of God and those of the world and of men are always invariably different. Since the fall of man the ways of man have always been in accord with those of the world, a system built to oppose the purposes of God for His creation.

> *8* "For my thoughts are not your thoughts,
> neither are your ways my ways,"

declares the Lord.
9 "As the heavens are higher than the earth,
so are my ways higher than your ways
and my thoughts than your thoughts."
(Isaiah 55:8-9)

The Lord says that the ways of men are different from His own set ways and that difference is as wide as the difference between heaven and earth. So to walk in the ways of God you must know them, and to know them you must learn them.

> Teach me your way, O LORD; lead me in a straight path because of my oppressor.
> (Psalm 27:11)

> He guides the humble in what is right and teaches them his way.
> (Psalm 25:9)

God must teach you His ways. Like the psalmist you have to cry out to him to teach you His ways and you must be willing to learn. To learn the ways of God He must show you. Therefore ask Him to show you His ways. Cry out to Him, *"Show me your ways, O Lord…"* (Psalm 25:4). As you spend time with Him in prayer, Bible reading, meditation etc. i.e. as you fulfill your call to fellowship you will be fulfilling your duty to walk in His ways.

Why you Must Walk in His Ways

- Because He so commands;
- Because His ways are perfect;
- Because it is a blessing to do so;

- Because He alone knows all that lies ahead.

Besides, He has not called you to do it on your own, but has given you His Holy Spirit to lead and guide you into His ways and teach you how to walk in His ways. Glory to His Name!

- Because the ways of men and of the world are deceitful (Psalm 119:29).

Such are the *"ways that seem right unto a man but at the end is destruction"* (Proverbs 12:14).

God's ways are outlined in His laws, decrees, precepts, statutes, principles and commands. As you walk in His ways, you are fulfilling your destiny.

To Love the Lord

Just as it is a duty for spouses to love one another so as creatures, and more so as children of the Most High God, are we to love Him. The question is *"how are we to love Him?"*

> Love the LORD your God with all your heart and with all your soul and with all your strength.
> (Deuteronomy 6:5)
>
> Love the Lord your God with all your heart and with all your soul and with all your mind and with all your strength.
> (Mark 12:30)

God gave you a heart, that you should love Him with it. So He says love Him with all your heart. Your heart here refers to your inner man. He wants a love that is true and comes from within. He will not accept a love which springs from anywhere else. It is with all your heart or nothing.

God gave you a soul, that you should love Him with it. So He says love Him with all your soul (will, mind and emotions).

As you love the Lord with your heart, you must allow your soul to be involved. Thinking often about Him, telling Him you love Him and deciding to love Him.

God gave you strength so you could love Him with your strength. This too is all or nothing.

Manifestations of the Love for God

Like the fear of the Lord, the love for God in our hearts has ways in which it manifests itself, as revealed in the scriptures.

i. Obedience

This is love for God: to obey His commands.
(1 John 5:3a)

If you love Me, you will obey what I command.
(John 14:15)

Obeying the word of God and the voice of God is the first and foremost way of showing love to Him. He who claims to love God and then lives in disobedience is the greatest liar. For such claims do not tie with the word of God.

ii. Sacrifice

16 This is how we know what love is: Jesus Christ laid down his life for us. And we ought to lay down our lives for our brothers. *17* If anyone has material possessions and sees his brother in need but has no pity on him, how can the love of God be in him? *18* Dear children, let us not love with words or tongue but with actions and in truth.
(1 John 3:16-18)

Love for God is manifested in sacrificing for the needs of others. It is manifested in pouring out ourselves for the sake of others. That is sacrifice. He uses the death of Christ Jesus as an example to appeal to you to manifest God's love in the same way. It says we ought to. This talks of an obligation, a duty which must be carried out. Sharing your resources and possessions with your brothers or sisters is one way of showing love for God.

iii. Love for your Brother

20 If anyone says, 'I love God,' yet hates his brother, he is a liar. For anyone who does not love his brother, whom he has seen, cannot love God, whom he has not seen. *21* And he has given us this command: Whoever loves God must also love his brother.
(1 John 4:20-21)

A third manifestation of love for God is love for your fellow man. You cannot separate them. The characteristics of true Christian love are outlined in 1 Corinthians 13:1-8.

These are the qualities of the love you should have.

iv. Feeding the Sheep and Lambs of Christ (see John 21:15-18)

Love for God is manifested in being part of the great commission to make disciples of all nations. It is shown in our commitment to build up and take care of the lambs and sheep of the Lord Jesus. Putting spiritual food within the reach of those who will otherwise not get it.

v. In not Loving the World

> Do not love the world or anything in the world. If anyone loves the world, the love of the Father is not in him.
> (1 John 2:15)

If you love the world, the love of the Father is not in you.

If you love the things of the world, the love of the Father is not in you. The greatest betrayal of lovelessness for God is by loving the world; its ways, values, standards, methods, offers etc. Does not the Word say anyone who makes friendship with the world becomes God's enemy? (James 4:4)

As you love the Lord you are fulfilling your destiny.

To Serve the Lord your God

Your fourth duty as a creation and more so as a child is to serve the Lord. How?

i. With all your Heart (Deuteronomy 10:12)

This talks of service that originates from the spirit of man, that which is in accord with God's purpose for you as an individual. Not service which is a result of gratification of the self-life. Wholehearted devotion is paramount in your service to the Lord (2 Chronicles 19:9).

ii. With all your Soul (Deuteronomy 10:12)

This talks of your will, emotions and mind being totally, completely and wholly involved in the service of the Lord. Emotions here talk of serving Him with joy, gladness etc.

iii. With Faithfulness (Joshua 24:14; see also 2 Chronicles 19:9)

To be faithful means to be trustworthy in the performance of duty. It means always being there whatever happens.

It talks of firm attachment to duty. Faithfulness is an indispensable virtue in acceptable service to God.

iv. With Willingness of Mind (1 Chronicles 28:9)

This is a readiness to do whatever the Lord asks you to do, where He asks you to do it, when He asks you to do it. This is what a willingness of heart and mind is about.

v. In the Fear of the Lord (2 Chronicles 19:9)

A man can serve with all his heart, with all his soul, with faithfulness and a willing mind for selfish reasons and ambitions. Every service to God must have as foundation, and must be crowned with the fear of the Lord; doing it for His Name's sake, His interest, His Kingdom, and His glory. That is true service.

The Danger of Pride in Service

As you serve the Lord, be careful not to glory in self. Your promotion can come from your service likewise your disqualification. The Lord is committed to share His glory with no other, not even you. About a servant of His, the Bible says,

> *12* When the Lord has finished all his work against Mount Zion and Jerusalem, he will say, "I will punish the king of Assyria for the willful pride of his heart and the haughty look in his eyes. *13* For he says:
> "By the strength of my hand I have done this,
> and by my wisdom, because I have understanding.
> I removed the boundaries of nations,
> I plundered their treasures;
> like a mighty one I subdued their kings."
> (Isaiah 10:12-13)

When God uses, there's need for self-abasement and self-effacement. God opposes all that is pride and haughtiness. The Assyrian was a rod in God's hand;

God sent him

God dispatched him.

A man can be called by God, chosen by God, sent by God, for a special purpose, yet God looks at intentions and motives (see Isaiah 10:7). It is a tragedy to go on God's errands with a secret motive and intent. Unless your goal is to do only that for which God sent you, you better not be a part of it.

To whom do you give glory for that which God is using you or for what He has accomplished through you? God is not only interested in what a man is at the time He is using Him but in what he becomes after God has used him. You can be greatly used of God today and thrown aside tomorrow if pride and haughtiness come in.

How then can you know when pride is present in that which you are doing for the Lord?

Elements of Pride

- Presumptuousness: *"because I did it yesterday I can do it better today"*.
- Strong self-will: wanting to do it your own way.
- Thinking in your heart *"I have done it"*.
- Saying in your heart or to others, *"but for me…"* or *"because I was there…"*
- Thinking or saying, *"This one cannot do it better than I"* or *"if it were me I'll do it better"*.
- The desire to be praised and hailed for *"doing it well"*.
- Looking down on others.
- Trying to exercise grace beyond your faith.
- Always seeing mistakes in what others do.

A good case study of what we are saying here is the king Uzziah (see 2 Chronicles 26).

He was a very successful king who knew prosperity and success in all domains of his life.

- He knew military success (vv 6-9, 11-14).
- He knew economic success (v 10).
- He knew scientific and technological success (v 15)

Why? Because, *"as long as he sought the Lord, God gave him success"*. His success never came through fraud, extortion or any such ungodly means but through earnest hard work.

Beware of Fame and Power

> The Ammonites brought tribute to Uzziah, and his fame spread as far as the border of Egypt, because he had become very powerful.
> (2 Chronicles 26:8)

> But after Uzziah became powerful, his pride led to his downfall. He was unfaithful to the LORD his God, and entered the temple of the LORD to burn incense on the altar of incense.
> (2 Chronicles 26:16)

Fame and power even when they are God-given, can become the source of a man's downfall if not properly handled. If God blesses you in ministry or whatever your calling or purpose may be, it becomes absolutely necessary to seek and receive from Him a heart that is humble. Humility is a must for your service to be accepted by God. Pride is the pathway to nothing but a great fall. Uzziah's pride as a result of his fame and power was manifested in the following ways:

i. Trying to Render Service beyond His Grace and Faith

Uzziah was not a priest, he was not called to offer sacrifices but his pride led him into this error to try to render service beyond his calling.

ii. Despising the God-ordained Ministry of Others

In trying to offer sacrifices, Uzziah was despising the God ordained ministry of the priest. He reached a point where he saw no need for the priest. He thought he could do it all alone.

iii. Despising the Authority of the Priest

Uzziah thought he was the alpha and omega of Israel in all domains. He refused heeding the warning and wise counsel of the priest for him to leave the temple.

- The proud man *"can and wants to do"* everything.
- The proud man *"can do everything better"*.
- The proud man always sees himself as *"anointed for every service"*.

God cannot allow you violate His ordinances, statutes, and principles no matter the degree of your success in ministry, or business or what ever your calling is. Labor to remain in your God-ordained sphere of service and influence.

- The proud man gets angry when confronted about his sin.

Let us avoid falling in the same error of becoming proud like Lucifer did and became eternally condemned. God opposes the proud. The easiest way to court opposition from the Almighty, Omniscient, and Omnipotent God is to harbor pride in the heart.

- Desire to be the highest.
- Desire to *"sit"* on others.

- Desire to take another's position, to overthrow others. (Compare Isaiah 14:13-15)

Acceptable Service

There's absolutely no reason to glory in self for any accomplishment whatsoever. It is God who uses you and who works through you. You just must see that unless God does something your efforts for that thing are useless. There are two possibilities for any child of God: to do things in his own strength or to do those same things with God's own strength (1 Pet 4: 11b). Once there is any trace of self-glory in that which you are doing, it is most likely you are acting in your own strength and such service cannot stand the test of time for *"the flesh profiteth nothing"*. When God's strength is used, the praise, the glory, honor and power invariably go back to God. You increasingly see yourself as nothing and God as everything.

> The Lord asks, "Does the axe raise itself above him who swings it, or the saw boast against him who uses it? As if a rod were to wield him who lifts it up, or a club brandish him who is not wood!"
> (Isaiah 10: 15)

There is no way you can use God's strength and serve and then give the glory to self and be free about it. The Spirit of God will surely convict you until you acknowledge that you are nothing but a vessel, which the Master in His sovereignty decided to use.

Let me ask you a question or two:
In whose strength have you been serving?

To who does the praise and glory and honor go after a successful accomplishment?

He who serves in God's strength is confident in the Lord, that he *"can do all things through Christ who strengthens"* him.

Did not the prophet Isaiah say, *"…all that we have accomplished you have done for us"* (Isaiah 26: 12b)?

It is all you've accomplished. Not some, not most, but all that you have accomplished. Without God you can do nothing, absolutely nothing (John 15: 5b); nothing big, nothing small, no matter how much you try. No matter how much you invest in the measure of time, energy, money and other resources. Unless you remain in vital union with Christ; uninterrupted fellowship and communion with your risen Lord, it is not only impossible that you do anything but you become useless and totally unfit for anything but the fire.

We see two extremes here for a child of God. The negative side of being able to do absolutely nothing without Christ and the positive side of being able to do everything through Christ who gives you strength. There is just one channel to receiving this strength; a vital union with The Vine–the Lord Jesus Christ. Anything, which takes or attempts to take you away from this uninterrupted communion ceases to be service and becomes spiritual suicide. May God open our eyes to be able to see in our lives how much suicide is being carried out under the canopy of service. The sad thing about such *"suicide mission"* is that we aren't dying for the Vine but from the Vine. What glory it is to die for the Vine and what horror it is to die from the Vine. Do you see the difference? As clear as night is from day! The pathway to effective service is to stay in a vital union with the Vine.

Why God Must Do it and not you.

"I know that everything God does will endure forever; nothing can be added to it and nothing taken from it. God does it so that men will revere him."
(Ecclesiastes 3:14)

i. Durability

The word *"endure"* here talks of the ability to resist and stay in the best condition with changing time and circumstances. God alone knows the circumstances which will surround what you are doing both in the near and distant future. He alone knows the needs that will arise many years from now. And when He does it He takes all these into consideration.

ii. What God Does is Final (see also Isaiah 43:13)

God is the greatest power, the greatest authority in this universe. He alone is infinitely wise. What He does He places His seal on it and therefore no one can change or alter it whether by addition or by subtraction. None can make it more effective by adding more wisdom to it.

iii. God Does everything to Reveal His Glory

One may do something to seek his own fame or honor but when God does it through you and for you it is *"so that man will revere Him"*. Yeah, His ultimate purpose is to reveal His glory to mankind.

iv. God alone Knows the Best Time for Everything

> There is a time for everything and a season for every activity under heaven.
>
> (Ecclesiastes 3:1).

There's a time interval within which anything has to be accomplished for it to have the greatest result. Only God knows what has to be done at which time. Why? Because *"He has made everything beautiful in it's own time"*. Out of it's own time it becomes ugly and without attraction. This places a responsibility on the one whom God must work with or work through to, through vital union with the Vine, *"understand the times and know that which has to be done"* at any given time.

As you labor to fulfill your destiny through serving the Lord, ensure that such service is void of pride and is acceptable before God.

To Observe the Lord's Commands

This fifth duty of yours is really a part of the first four. As you fear the Lord, as you love the Lord, as you walk in His ways, and as you serve Him in truth and in sincerity you are observing His commands.

Observing His commands here talks of living according to the Word of God. Practicing that which the Bible recommends. I'll write more on this in my book *"Secrets to practical living"* in the section on practical Christianity.

Fulfill your destiny by fulfilling your duty!

In these next sections, I'll want to help you first of all to discover Satan's strategy to destroying a vision, how you can launch a counter offensive in case your vision has been stolen, how to receive a vision in case you've never had one and lastly, how to accomplish your vision.

A TWENTY MINUTES STOP

✣ Points to Meditate on

a. God has made His infinite grace available to enable you, and His Spirit to lead you into doing His will.

b. Evil is anything that cannot stand the presence of God; anything that is against His revealed will.

c. You must be willing to learn from both your mistakes and those of others.

d. The fear of the Lord brings you to a point where your desires become one with His. You begin to long for nothing but that which He desires for you and wants of you and for you.

e. The ways of God and those of men and of the world are invariably different.

f. The greatest betrayal of lovelessness towards God is by loving the world.

g. God is not only interested in a man when He is using him but in what a man becomes after God has used him.

h. The easiest way to court opposition from God is to harbor pride in the heart.

i. The pathway to effective service is to stay in vital union with the Vine.

✣ Decisions

✣ Heartcry

"Thank you for making Your grace so abundantly available to me, Father. With such abundant grace, I resolve to shun evil, to learn from my mistakes and those of others. Bring me to the point where I'll become one with You in everything. Help me develop a humble heart even as I stay in vital union with You."

Chapter Five

SATAN'S STRATEGY TO DESTROY VISION

Everything that has its origin from God, anything that will serve the interests of the kingdom of God, anything that brings blessing to God's beloved human race becomes a target of the hater of the souls of men. When you are working to fulfill that which God created you for, you become a prime target of the enemy. His goal is to destroy your vision and abort your destiny. That is why this chapter will be dedicated to exposing the devil's strategy to destroy vision. Stick with me a little as we uncover Satan's strategy to destroy vision.

> And I answered the king, "If it pleases the king and if your servant has found favor in his sight, let him send me to the city in Judah where my fathers are buried so that I can rebuild it."
>
> (Nehemiah 2:5)

This was the vision of Nehemiah by the time he was leaving this foreign land to go to Judah. Let us now see how Satan tried to destroy this vision of his and that of Ezra.

Disguise

To disguise means any of the following:

- To change the appearance of;
- To hide or conceal the identity;
- To obscure or cover up the actual nature or character by false representation.

> *1* When the enemies of Judah and Benjamin heard that the exiles were building a temple for the Lord, the God of Israel, *2* they came to Zerubbabel and to the heads of the families and said, Let us help you build because, like you, we seek your God and have been sacrificing to him since the time of Esarhaddon king of Assyria, who brought us here.
> *3* But Zerubbabel, Jeshua and the rest of the heads of the families of Israel answered, You have no part with us in building a temple to our God. We alone will build it for the Lord, the God of Israel, as King Cyrus, the king of Persia, commanded us.
> (Ezra 4:1-3)

The devil has never come openly on his missions. He has always disguised, and always pretended.

These enemies of Judah said three things

1. Let us help: There are some who can pretend to be helping but what they are doing is actually scattering.

They seem to give a helping hand outwardly but inside, how they wish all will fail. They build with a secret desire to see it crumble.

Are you sincere in the helping hand you appear to give?

For how long have you covered the real you?

2. We seek your God.
3. We have been sacrificing to Him.

These people appeared to be earnest in their request to give a helping hand. Now turn with me to the book of kings lets see how they worshipped this God they claimed to worship

> *29* Nevertheless, each national group made its own gods in the several towns where they settled, and set them up in the shrines the people of Samaria had made at the high places. *30* The men from Babylon made Succoth Benoth, the men from Cuthah made Nergal, and the men from Hamath made Ashima; *31* the Avvites made Nibhaz and Tartak, and the Sepharvites burned their children in the fire as sacrifices to Adrammelech and Anammelech, the gods of Sepharvaim. *32* They worshiped the Lord, but they also appointed all sorts of their own people to officiate for them as priests in the shrines at the high places. *33* They worshiped the Lord, but they also served their own gods in accordance with the customs of the nations from which they had been brought.
>
> (2 Kings 17:29-33)

Are you serving Jehovah only or Jehovah and some other idol?

Are you seeking Him only or Him plus whatever?

Anybody who serves God plus some other thing is an enemy to God, and thus to God's people. Though such may pretend to help build the work of God, all such can do is scatter and wish that all will crumble.

- Pretenders have no part with God's people
- Oh that we are quick to discern pretenders and put them aside.
- For how long will you keep two faces? For how long will you pretend and continue to scatter that which God's people are building?

Oh that you may take off your mask

Oh that the east wind of the Lord carries away that mask and exposes the real you.

- How long will you pretend to be there while in your heart you wish you were never there?

Shall we dare to say these enemies of Judah had good intentions but their divided worship of God and idols disqualified them from being partakers in this great project of restoring the temple?

My heart cry is that vision bearers will become more discerning than ever before so as to identify the enemies even in their disguise and like the returning exiles say to them, *"You have no part with us..."*

When these enemies of Judah came, they followed the right procedure. They did not just go and start giving a helping hand but went to the leaders – Zerubabel and the heads of the families (V2). What am I trying to say? The enemy understands protocol and in most cases he will undergo the right procedures just to arrive where he wants. Those whom we usually accuse to be rebels might not be our real enemies. The real enemies come in disguise, in false humility, in false submission, respecting all protocol. It is time, by the power of the Holy Spirit, leaders begin to discern beneath the surface of things. It is time that leaders begin to decipher motives behind offers and appearances.

It is not enough that someone tells you he or she is a seeker of God or has been sacrificing to the Lord God of Israel. Does the life of the person bear testimony as a God seeker? Do his priorities proclaim it loudly? Are his values Christian values? What are the things, which give him pleasure? What are his standards and ways?

These are only surface questions that will help us know who we can trust but again and again, we can only rely on the Spirit of the Living God to bear testimony in our hearts of whom to trust.

Many visions have been destroyed not by those who seemed to have opposed it outrightly from without but by those who appeared to have been in total support at the very beginning but after gaining enough grounds, to cause the greatest havoc, took off the mask of disguise to accomplish what they actually came for.

Did not the Lord of glory warn us about this?

> Watch out for false prophets. They come to you in sheep's clothing, but inwardly they are ferocious wolves.
> (Matthew 7: 15)

He said, *"Watch out for..."* It means we need to be observant, examine closely and allow the Spirit to give approval. Why? Because they shall come in sheep clothing. They shall appear as sheep whereas they actually are not. Why? So they can have their way easily among the sheep.

In Luke 10:3, He told them *"I am sending you out as lambs among wolves".*

Yeah, He was sending them out, so care had to be taken because it was quite obvious they were going to encounter wolves-enemies from without.

Here our problem is the wolves-in-sheep-clothing. It was also the cry of the apostle Paul when it was time for him to depart from Ephesus.

> **29** I know that after I leave, savage wolves will come in among you and will not spare the flock. **30** Even from your own number men will arise and distort the truth in order to draw away disciples after them. **31** So be on your guard! Remember that for three years I never stopped warning each of you night and day with tears.
> (Acts 20: 29-31)

The savage wolves would come in as sheep and from among them rise to destroy the flock. What pains my heart is the phrase *"Even from your own number..."* meaning they had always been there but the right opportunity had not come for them to have their mission accomplished. What was his advice to the elders in Ephesus? *"Be on your guard".*

The Lord said *"Watch out for..."* Paul said, " *Be on your guard"*, the wise person takes heed.

Distraction (Disorientation)

"To distract means to draw or divert in a different direction or in various directions..."

1 When word came to Sanballat, Tobiah, Geshem the Arab and the rest of our enemies that I had rebuilt the wall and not a gap was left in it–though up to that time I had not set the doors in the gates– *2* Sanballat and Geshem sent me this message: "Come, let us meet together in one of the villages on the plain of Ono."
But they were scheming to harm me; *3* so I sent messengers to them with this reply: "I am carrying on a great project and cannot go down. Why should the work stop while I leave it and go down to you?" *4* Four times they sent me the same message, and each time I gave them the same answer.
(Nehemiah 6: 1-4)

Here is another great weapon in Satan's strategy to destroy vision–distraction and disorientation. When the devil wants to destroy a man he seeks to divert the man's attention from the focus, from the real thing. The one who must succeed is the one who must persistently refuse to yield to the pressure to get distracted or disoriented.

What was the mission of Samballat and Geshem? Nothing but to get Nehemiah distracted from his vision. At this time, their weapon number one, disguise, had failed in the case of the temple, so they decided to use another weapon from their arsenal-distraction.

"Come let us meet together in one of the villages on the plain of Ono", was their message. What for? Why? Was the plain of Ono

part of Nehemiah's vision? Certainly not! The enemy realized the best way to destroy the vision was to have it slowed down, because the vision bearer was not there to carry his people to completion of the project as a result of his being distracted.

At this time, the project of rebuilding the wall was near completion, all that was lacking was the setting up of the doors in the gates, but the enemy had not given up, they did all to get Nehemiah distracted from the vision.

A man can be doing something, yet in a distracted state. It will not usually mean a complete abandoning of the work. It mostly will mean, not having the whole resources focused and in place.

Like we said before, the Lord asked us to watch; the apostle Paul asked us to be on guard, so as to unmask the disguise of the enemy. So the enemy now employs a new weapon, distraction. If there's one thing a distracted person cannot do is watch or be on guard.

Distraction doesn't just get you off focus from the vision, it gets you off guard against the enemy and before long great havoc is caused.

You know, God has always meant for us to live this Christian life on the mountain. But like Lot, many of us have chosen to live on the plain—the place of the ordinary. When Lot was delivered out of Sodom he was asked to run to the mountain but he objected and decided to settle on the plain, in the small village of Zoar. You know what followed.

The enemy wanted to employ the same strategy in the case of Nehemiah, to get him down from his mountain of total commitment to the vision, to the plain of Ono to honor an appointment with the enemy. There is nothing in the plain worth your attention, especially at the price of suspending that great project of the building of His Kingdom, seeing His will done in the lives of countless individuals.

How many of us have abandoned our God-given projects, to partake in life on the plain. Being engaged in activities of no consequence?

Are we not honoring the enemy's invitations in some of the things we are now doing? Are we not disoriented?

Let me ask you a question. Are you on the walls putting up the doors in the gates or on the plain of Ono?

Nehemiah understood that this was a weapon in the hands of his own enemies so his reply was,

"I am carrying on a great project and can not go down. Why should the work stop while I leave it and go down to you?"

That was indeed an apt reply. He knew work could not continue up while he was down. In spite of the persistence of his enemies, he refused going down.

The enemy knows that a distracted person is unfit for God's Kingdom. Did not our Lord say *"Anyone who lets himself be distracted from the work I plan for him is not fit for the Kingdom of heaven"*. (Luke 9:62, Living Bible)

"Anyone who lets himself...", so its a matter of personal choice, to refuse all distractions, to resist the enemy each time or to give in to distraction and be self-disqualified.

Again, Let me ask, "Are you at the wall or on the plain of Ono?

This takes us to the next weapon in his strategy.

Displacement (Disconnection)

Nothing creates an open door for the enemy into the life and vision of a man or woman like being in the wrong place for whatever reason. The enemies of God's people knew that it was impossible to harm the vision bearer while he was at his place of work. They schemed to have him distracted and ultimately displaced so they could harm him. (Nehemiah 6 : 2b)

The devil knows it is impossible for him to harm you while you are *"In place",* so he labors to get you displaced.

A man can be destined for blessings and for greatness but once displaced, he is taken out of the position for blessing. Let us look at some examples of people who were displaced and hence got themselves in trouble.

Dinah

> *1* Now Dinah, the daughter Leah had borne to Jacob, went out to visit the women of the land. *2* When Shechem son of Hamor the Hivite, the ruler of that area, saw her, he took her and violated her.
> (Genesis 34:1-2)

Dinah went out to visit the women of the land. Someone might well put it in modern day terms, she went out for a stroll. Out of the protection of her father and brothers alone in the neighborhood among the girls of the land. She thus found herself in the wrong place amongst the wrong people. This created an open door for the enemy to attack. How many young girls have found themselves in deep trouble because they were at the wrong place, out of the covering of a loving family. Look, there's nothing out there for you to see, there's no good thing out of the home of your heavenly Father nor of your earthly parents for you to experience. It might seem appealing, and your parents who are doing all to protect your interest may now appear to be your enemies because they won't allow you go out there. The best you can do for yourself is to hearken to them.

Your destruction can come from the very thing that appears to be innocent. It might be just a visit; just an outing in the wrong place with the wrong people and your whole future is destroyed. How many young girls have found themselves in the hands of a Shechem who has raped and abused them but in fear and shame have refused to raise any alarm. Too many of them are suffering in silence from the hands of the sons of Hamor.

Hamor means an ass and many daughters of princes of the Most High God have been abused and tormented by sons of asses. When someone is at the wrong place out of protection she becomes far stupid than an ass, such that even sons of an ass can take advantage of her. Is it any wonder that Dinah is never mentioned again in the scriptures? Her destiny was marred.

Judah

> *1* At that time, Judah left his brothers and went down to stay with a man of Adullam named Hirah. *2* There Judah met the daughter of a Canaanite man named Shua. He married her and lay with her.
>
> (Genesis 38:1-2)

Here again we find another case of someone, this time a young man, at the wrong place with the wrong person. Judah, decided to leave home, for whatever reason, out of the protection of loving parents and family to stay with a man of Adullam. Adullam means refuge. Surely Judah thought he could find refuge with Hirah. He was seeking refuge from the great sin of selling their brother Joseph to slavery. So he thought the best thing was to go away from home. Many young people who run away from home usually do so from rebellion or guilt. They think they can find refuge away from home, the place that is meant to be refuge – refuge from sin, refuge from the enemy, refuge from bad friends – and in doing so expose themselves to the very things their parents are trying to protect them from. Here Judah married the daughter of a Cannanite named Shua. Shua means prosperity. I am quite sure that Judah thought by getting married to the daughter of prosperity he too, away from home, will become prosperous. But did this girl bring him prosperity? The events, which followed, show she didn't. Instead there was one calamity after another. What appears to bring prosperity usually does not.

> *My dear friend, there's no prosperity for you, out of the home of your heavenly Father. Do not let guilt displace you, else you fall into the hands of a Canaanite woman.*

We can go on and talk about David who was at the wrong place and fell into the sin of adultery. We can also talk of Jacob who instead of being at Bethel was at Shechem and became an idolater.

What about the prodigal son who thought life could best be lived out of home, out of the care of a loving father?

The lesson has been quite clear for he or she who has an open heart. The one who must remain blessed and accomplish his vision must be in the right place.

Discouragement (Demoralization)

1 When Sanballat heard that we were rebuilding the wall, he became angry and was greatly incensed. He ridiculed the Jews, *2* and in the presence of his associates and the army of Samaria, he said, "What are those feeble Jews doing? Will they restore their wall? Will they offer sacrifices? Will they finish in a day? Can they bring the stones back to life from those heaps of rubble–burned as they are?"
3 Tobiah the Ammonite, who was at his side, said, "What they are building–if even a fox climbed up on it, he would break down their wall of stones!"
(Nehemiah 4:1-3)

Then the peoples around them set out to discourage the people of Judah and make them afraid to go on building.
(Ezra 4:4)

Another great weapon in the hands of the enemy is discouragement. There are many ways by which he can accomplish this purpose but his ultimate goal is to get us discouraged. Before we continue, let us for a moment look at the ways by which these enemies set out to bring discouragement. We shall dwell on the passage cited above in Nehemiah.

Magnification of Weakness

"What are those feeble Jews doing?"

These people set out to point at the weakness of the Jews. They aimed at reminding the Jews of their inability to defend themselves against their enemies.

The devil does the same today. He tends to magnify our weaknesses before us, to let us know we are not the right people for the very job God has given us. What matters is that the One who chose to give you the vision knew and knows you too well to have made a mistake. It's all on the basis of His choice.

Magnification of the Difficulty of the Task

"Will they restore their wall? Will they offer sacrifices? Will they finish in a day?"

Their goal was to let the Jews get their focus on the difficulty of what they were doing. There is no task without difficulties but what Satan does is he tries to misrepresent the difficulties, making them too great to be overcome.

Did the Jews say their goal was to finish in a day? Certainly not! The enemy was trying to accuse them of what actually was inexistent.

Causing you to See the "Impossibilities"

"Can they bring the stones back to life..."

God calls us at times to do the impossible with respect to us humans. As long as we look at the impossibility we get discouraged. But once our eyes are on Him with whom *"all things are possible"* we get going.

A man can continue to do something but in utter discouragement. Once a thing is done in a discouraged condition the results are ineffective and unstable. If Nehemiah and his team got discouraged, then what the enemies said about the wall rebuilt in such condition would be true. That *"what they are rebuilding even if a fox climbs on it, he would break down their wall of stone!"*

Can you imagine a wall of stone being broken down by a fox? It shows that what we build does not just depend on the material we use but also on the state of our mind when building. It is for that reason God told Joshua again and again not to be discouraged because no permanent victory can be won in a state of discouragement.

Dismay

5 Then, the fifth time, Sanballat sent his aide to me with the same message, and in his hand was an unsealed letter 6 in which was written:
"'It is reported among the nations–and Geshem says it is true–that you and the Jews are plotting to revolt, and therefore you are building the wall. Moreover, according to these reports you are about to become their king 7 and

have even appointed prophets to make this proclamation about you in Jerusalem: 'There is a king in Judah!' Now this report will get back to the king; so come, let us confer together."

8 I sent him this reply: "Nothing like what you are saying is happening; you are just making it up out of your head."

9 They were all trying to frighten us, thinking, "Their hands will get too weak for the work, and it will not be completed."

But I prayed, "Now strengthen my hands."

(Nehemiah 6:5 – 9)

The ultimate purpose of the enemy in trying to discourage you in that which you are doing is not for you to continue doing it in a state of discouragement but to bring you to a state of dismay; a condition where a man becomes too discouraged to continue work. This is usually done through intimidation and accusations whether they are false or true. These people tried to distract Nehemiah, to no avail. They set out to displace him, to no avail, for Nehemiah would not leave his place of work. Now they set out to discourage him but to no avail. And so the next weapon was to get them stop work. How? Through intimidation, bad report, and false accusations. Do you see their accusation confirmed by Geshem who was also an enemy? Satan will rally all his forces to oppose that which you must accomplish for God. However, what counts is not how many witnesses the devil rallies against you but who is it that stands with you. And for sure we have someone who always stands with His own. Nehemiah never got dismayed.

Division

We deal with an enemy who never gives up until the final judgment shall be passed on him. He seeks to employ daily, new weapons with more devastating potentials where former ones did not work.

One of his most used and most effective weapons is that of division. Most often we have thought of division as amongst people or things, but here I will use the word to mean di-vision. The easiest way the devil has used to destroy vision is through disorientation and sometimes displacement to bring about two visions. To better put forth this point, let's turn to a very interesting passage in the Book.

> *16* Now two prostitutes came to the king and stood before him. *17* One of them said, "My lord, this woman and I live in the same house. I had a baby while she was there with me. *18* The third day after my child was born, this woman also had a baby. We were alone; there was no one in the house but the two of us.
> *19* "During the night this woman's son died because she lay on him. *20* So she got up in the middle of the night and took my son from my side while I your servant was asleep. She put him by her breast and put her dead son by my breast. *21* The next morning, I got up to nurse my son–and he was dead! But when I looked at him closely in the morning light, I saw that it wasn't the son I had borne."
> *22* The other woman said, "No! The living one is my son; the dead one is yours."
> But the first one insisted, "No! The dead one is yours; the living one is mine." And so they argued before the king.

23 The king said, "This one says, 'My son is alive and your son is dead,' while that one says, 'No! Your son is dead and mine is alive.'"
24 Then the king said, "Bring me a sword." So they brought a sword for the king. *25* He then gave an order: "Cut the living child in two and give half to one and half to the other."
26 The woman whose son was alive was filled with compassion for her son and said to the king, "Please, my lord, give her the living baby! Don't kill him!"
But the other said, "Neither I nor you shall have him. Cut him in two!"
27 Then the king gave his ruling: "Give the living baby to the first woman. Do not kill him; she is his mother"
28 When all Israel heard the verdict the king had given, they held the king in awe, because they saw that he had wisdom from God to administer justice."
(1 Kings 3:6-28)

If Satan cannot steal completely that which God has given a man he exchanges it with something similar but fake. Many who started with a God-given vision at some point ignorantly abandon their true pursuit for a counterfeit stuff. Why? Because at some point the vision became two; one real and one fake, and the devil took away the real thing.

Here we find two ladies, the first one and her child represent the vision bearer and his vision, the second represents the devil and a counterfeit vision. We see that there was an exchange, unknown to the vision bearer. When? At midnight!

Midnight is a time when a man has stopped working and fast asleep, a time when people are off-guard. The enemy will not come while you are watching but when you have ceased to watch, the time you are off-guard.

When this evil woman took the other's living child, she did not put her dead child at some other place, but at the woman's breast. In other words there was a replacement. When Satan exchanges, he puts the false thing in the same position as the authentic and you'll continue to hold the fake as dear to you. While asleep, this woman continued to hold the fake baby in her very bosom. When Satan cannot steal, he exchanges what you have with something fake, in a state of spiritual slumber.

Once a man stops nursing that which God gave him, Satan takes advantage of the situation and brings in something dead, and in slumber, that man may attempt to nurse the dead thing. Until this woman awoken from her deep sleep, she kept holding on to something which was dead. Many people need to awaken from their state of spiritual slumber, to examine what they have in their hands.

Does that which you have appear dead? You've awaken from slumber and found that what you now hold is a dead thing. Dead with respect to the interests of God, dead with respect to the perishing souls of men.

Is there life in that which you're holding to?

My fear is that many vision bearers are now holding to something dead, unknown to them. Oh that the morning may dawn for all, so that in attempting to nurse their vision they'll see it's something dead.

It takes a man's real spiritual alertness to recognize that what he now holds is not alive but dead. If the woman had gotten up without attempting to nurse her baby, she would not have known that it was now something dead.

That thing you're now pursuing might not be what God originally gave you. That dead thing you are holding on to is not your own!

There is need for close examination of that which a man holds to see if it actually is what he should be holding. The dead baby and the living one were both babies born about the same time. During periods of slumber things do actually change without a man knowing and he may awaken and assume that things were still the same meanwhile the difference is indeed as wide as life and death. When Samson awoken from his state of slumber in the laps of compromise, he was unaware of what had become of him. He was presumptuous not to examine himself to see if he was the same person. Spiritual slumber is like a soldier sleeping in the battlefront.

Have you taken time to closely examine that which you are now holding to? Or do you assume that all is but normal. For how long have you been in a state of spiritual slumber? Is it not time to get up? Is it still midnight for you? Have you not seen that there has been a di-vision?

Destruction

The Lord Jesus said, *"The thief comes only to steal to kill and destroy"* (John 10:10a) Who is the thief? Satan! We just said that when Satan cannot steal he kills by exchanging what you have with something fake, with the ultimate purpose to destroy.

In our passage in 1 Kings the final aim of this evil woman was to have the baby destroyed. She asked that the living baby be divided into two. In other words she wanted it destroyed. We said the two babies represent two visions of which one is always authentic and living and the other, counterfeit and dead. The enemy's purpose is to destroy the authentic.

Have you found out that your vision has been replaced? Take the case to the King and He surely will give the verdict in your favor.

A TEN-MINUTES STOP

✣ **Points to Meditate on**

a. Divided worship between God and anything in your life disqualifies you from God's purpose for your life.

b. If you must succeed, you must persistently refuse to yield to pressure to get you distracted and disoriented.

c. There's nothing worth your attention on the plain, at the price of suspending your God-given task.

d. A man can be destined for blessings and for greatness but once displaced he is taken out of the position for blessing.

e. Many who started with a God-given vision at some point ignorantly abundoned their true pursuit for something fake.

f. Once a man stops nurturing that which God gives him, satan takes advantage and exchanges it for something fake.

✣ **Decisions**

....

....

....

✤ Heartcry

"Lord, I ask for an undivided heart, wholly, completely and totally given to you. I refuse to yield to any pressure to get me off focus. Help me Lord to continually nurture what you have given me (or will give me) and to hold on to it."

Your Counter Strategy

Recognize your Enemy

The very first step to a counter offensive is to recognize your enemy in disguise, recognize his weapons and strongholds, recognize the sources of distraction, recognize his methods of getting you discouraged and dismayed, and recognize the state in which you are.

There must be some recognition of the enemy and his schemes and devices. We already mentioned some in the first part of this teaching.

Today, Like in the days of Paul, there's one great source of distraction and trap of the enemy—the quest for riches by vision bearers.

> People who want to get rich fall into temptation and a trap and into many foolish and harmful desires that plunge men into ruin and destruction. For the love of money is a root of all kinds of evil. Some people, eager for money, have wandered from the faith and pierced themselves with many grieves.
> (I Tim 6: 9, 10)

The desire for wealth does the following

- It causes you to fall into temptation;
- It gets you into a trap (of the devil);
- It gets you into many foolish desires;
- It gets you into many harmful desires;
- It plunges you into ruin and destruction;
- It causes you to wonder from the faith;
- It causes you to pierce yourself with many grieves.

Thus we see that the number one enemy to the maturing of a vision is the desire for riches and the love of money. The devil gets a lot of people to compromise their vision for something different because of the desire for wealth. Others abandon the vision to go for vocations with financial security.

In the parable of the sower, some seed did not mature because of life's worries, riches and pleasure. These can be taken for visions which die immature because they are choked by riches and the desire and love for it.

To properly deal with your enemy, you've got to recognize his manifestations and guises:

1. Love for riches

2. Love for pleasure
3. Love for fame

Like we said, after recognizing, the next step is to keep guard and be watchful.

Other enemies to your vision include:

- Doubt,
- fear,
- imitation
- laziness,
- procrastination,
- love of power,
- competition.

Renounce, Recollect and Realign

Now we said, another of his weapons is distraction. Have you found that the enemy has distracted you? Are you investing time and energy and other resources where you are not supposed to, in a thing that is of no benefit to His kingdom or better still to your vision? If so, you've got to first of all renounce those things, which now act as a distraction. You've got to put them aside by all means. This renunciation is indispensable. Without it there is no way to come out of the distraction. After this indispensable renunciation the next thing is to recollect your thoughts, yourself and resources. Why must there be this recollection? Because a distracted person always scatters his thoughts and resources which he otherwise would invest in his vision. Distraction saps away useful thoughts and resources and a man is left with little to invest into that which God has called him to.

Just like the renunciation is painful but indispensable, the recollection also is difficult and indispensable. Unless there is this recollection, the renunciation avails to nothing. Recollection breaks any link between the distraction and you. The recollection can span from emotional, financial, psychological, social and even spiritual. Some people are distracted emotionally, others financial, others in their mind or thought life, some in their relationships and others in their spiritual activities. For some it may be in two or more domains.

After recollection, there must be realignment, this time of the will or reorientation of the will. Remember we talked of disorientation hence there must be a reorientation—looking and moving in the right and original direction. Unless there is this realignment of the will in the right direction, the recollection will produce little or no results. The realignment is like investing the recollected resources, time, etc in the one thing – your God-given vision. My brother this realignment has to be daily, nay, hourly, or it becomes pretty difficult. It's like having your hand constantly and continuously on the steering wheel to put the vehicle on track before it gets out of control.

Reposition and Reconnect

The third weapon in his strategy, we said, is displacement or de-positioning and disconnection. Once a man gets de-positioned from the right place for whatever reason he gets disconnected from the source of his strength, protection, provision and direction. The one who recognizes having been displaced or de-positioned has no option but to reposition himself in the place of blessings. A man can be earmarked for blessings but just being at the wrong place gets him disconnected from the very source of blessing. You may wonder why I am talking of repositioning. It is because something can be in the right place yet in the wrong position. However, there must be a replacement before there can be any repositioning for those who have been displaced.

Let's turn to scripture for an example to better illustrate this fact. It is in the account of Jacob who found himself in the wrong place Paddan Aram instead of being in the land of promise. Being in the wrong place, he used underhanded means to get his wealth like he had done to steal Esau's blessing. At a certain point in time the LORD appeared to him saying *"Go back to the land of your fathers and to your relatives, and I will be with you"*. (Genesis 31:3)

In other words *"Jacob, do not think of settling here, it is the wrong place. You've got to go to the right place"*. Though Jacob obeyed and moved to the land of his fathers, he relocated on the wrong position–Shechem instead of Bethel, and there at Shechem he was separated from God and his family became involved in idolatry. You know what happened at Shechem and the LORD asked him to move to the right position–Bethel–the house of God, the place of the altar, the place of revelation, sacrifice and worship.

> *1* Then God said to Jacob, "Go up to Bethel and settle there, and build an altar there to God, who appeared to you when you were fleeing from your brother Esau."
> *2* So Jacob said to his household and to all who were with him, "Get rid of the foreign gods you have with you, and purify yourselves and change your clothes. *3* Then come, let us go up to Bethel, where I will build an altar to God, who answered me in the day of my distress and who has

been with me wherever I have gone." *4* So they gave Jacob all the foreign gods they had and the rings in their ears, and Jacob buried them under the oak at Shechem. *5* Then they set out, and the terror of God fell upon the towns all around them so that no one pursued them.

6 Jacob and all the people with him came to Luz (that is, Bethel) in the land of Canaan. *7* There he built an altar, and he called the place El Bethel, because it was there that God revealed himself to him when he was fleeing from his brother.

8 Now Deborah, Rebekah's nurse, died and was buried under the oak below Bethel. So it was named Allon Bacuth.

9 After Jacob returned from Paddan Aram, God appeared to him again and blessed him. *10* God said to him, "Your name is Jacob, but you will no longer be called Jacob; your name will be Israel." So he named him Israel.

11 And God said to him, "I am God Almighty; be fruitful and increase in number. A nation and a community of nations will come from you, and kings will come from your body. *12* The land I gave to Abraham and Isaac I also give to you, and I will give this land to your descendants after you." *13* Then God went up from him at the place where he had talked with him.

14 Jacob set up a stone pillar at the place where God had talked with him, and he poured out a drink offering on it; he also poured oil on it.

(Genesis 35:1-14)

Though now in the right place, Jacob was in the wrong position, which brought about the disconnection from God. This disconnection was manifested in idolatry and murder by two of his sons. Until there was this command to reposition, Jacob could not have given the order for an end to all idolatry in his household. Repositioning demands cleansing and separation.

Once there was the repositioning, there were steps to reconnect.

"There he built an altar and he called the place EL Bethel..."

For there to be reconnection, there must be the building of an altar – the place of sacrifice, prayer and worship in the life of an individual.

Now take a look at verse 9. God appeared to him and blessed him only after he returned from Paddan Aram. My friend, there must be a replacement, a repositioning and a reconnection.

Reliance and Renewal

We said discouragement is another weapon in the hand of the enemy to destroy vision. We said he does this principally through the following:

1. Magnification of your weaknesses
2. Magnification of the difficulty
3. Causing you to see the impossibilities

And he may just be letting you see why you should rely more on God, though he may not know. As children of God, the obstacles of the devil on the way to our destiny are just stepping-stones to our God-ordained heights. More than ever we tend not to rely on ourselves but on Him who called us. In the face of discouragement what you must do is rely on Him who is not just the source of your strength but your very strength. Never rely on your capacities; never rely on your abilities; never rely even on your zeal but on Him only.

> **5** Not that we are competent in ourselves to claim anything for ourselves, but our competence comes from God. **6** He has made us competent as ministers of a new covenant—not of the letter but of the Spirit; for the letter kills, but the Spirit gives life.
> (2 Corinthians 3:5-6)

You have no competence on your own. Your competence comes from God who has made you a minister of the New Covenant. And so you rely on Him and nothing else. Like Nehemiah, in the face of discouragement, turn to your God and pray, *"Now strengthen my hands"* (Nehemiah 6: 9). Tell yourself daily:

"My competence comes from the Lord".

Does not the word of the Lord say,

> **14** Therefore, since we have a great high priest who has gone through the heavens, Jesus the Son of God, let us hold firmly to the faith we profess. **15** For we do not have a high priest who is unable to sympathize with our weaknesses, but we have one who has been tempted in every way, just as we are—yet was without sin. **16** Let us then approach the throne of grace with confidence, so that we may receive mercy and find grace to help us in our time of need.
> (Hebrews 4:14-16)

- The Lord Jesus sympathizes with your weakness;
- You can approach His throne with confidence;
- You will receive mercy in times of error
- You will find grace to help you in time of need.

Hallelujah! Won't you just lift up your hands and bless His holy Name and thank Him for all He is to you?

So we rely on Him and then renew our strength daily.

It took me time to decide how to place this point whether as Renewal and Reliance or Reliance and Renewal. Then I realized both would mean the same thing. The more we rely, the more we renew and we rely by renewing.

So while we ensure that we are relying on Him we get to renew our strength. In a case where you are already discouraged then first get to renew, then rely. How do you renew?

> *29* He gives strength to the weary
> and increases the power of the weak.
> *30* Even youths grow tired and weary,
> and young men stumble and fall.
> (Isaiah 40:29-30)

God gives strength to the weary and increases the power of the weak. He has nothing to offer the man who is so full of self-power but has everything to offer the weak. Yes He has everything to offer the weak.

At any time, all that you should present to God is your emptiness, your weariness, your weakness, and your sinfulness. God is interested in how weary you are so He can give you strength. He does not give strength to the strong.

How weary are you for God to give you strength? If God were to pour out His strength how much can you receive? Weariness comes through hard work and expending of energy.

God is also interested in how weak you are so He can increase your power. Are you weak enough to qualify for God's power? Weakness talks of a deficiency in Power.

Are you too weak for the task God has given you? This is just the right reason to turn to God; He is so willing to empower you.

How can it be that God is interested in he who provides Him with weakness (Deficiency in strength, experience and durability) so He can impart to him His strength (power to be and do and bear)?

Because this has always been his way of working. Do you remember Moses? What about Gideon? And Saul, son of Kish?

Can you recall each of their response when God first called them?

Moses said, *"Who am I, that I should go to the pharaoh and bring the Israelites out of Egypt?"*

> Oh lord, I have never been eloquent, neither in the past nor since you have spoken to your servant. I am slow of speech and tongue.
> (Exodus 3:11; Exodus 4:10).

Gideon said, *"How can I save Israel? My clan is the weakest in Manasseh, and I am the least in my family."* (Judges 6:15)

Saul said,

> But am I not a Benjamite, from the smallest tribe of Israel, and is not my clan the least of all clans of the tribe of Benjamin? Why should you say such a thing to me?
>
> (1 Samuel 9:21)

> **27** But God chose the foolish things of the world to shame the wise; God chose the weak things of the world to shame the strong. **28** He chose the lowly things of this world and the despised things—and the things that are not—to nullify the things that are, **29** so that no one may boast before him.
>
> (1 Corinthians 1:27-29)

He chose the foolish things;

He chose the weak things;

He chose the low things;

He chose the things that are not.

Why?

So no one may boast before Him.

Have you become too strong for God to give you any more strength?

Have you become too experienced for God to teach you?

Have you become too able to carry your burdens?

Have you become too sophisticated for God to use you?

Have you become too noble and honored for God to choose you any longer?

How do you renew your strength?

> But those who wait on the LORD
> Shall renew their strength;
> They shall mount up with wings like eagles,
> They shall run and not be weary,
> They shall walk and not faint.
> (Isaiah 40: 31, NKJV)

By waiting on the LORD.

Results

- You shall renew your strength;
- You shall mount up with wings as eagles;
- You shall run and not be weary;
- You shall walk and not faint.

There is an indispensable need for constant and continuous reliance and renewal. God help us!

Revival

While somebody may be discouraged, he may well still continue to act in the state of discouragement. But someone who is dismayed has been deprived not just of courage but even of the ability to act. Thus while the remedy for a discouraged or demoralized person is reliance and renewal, the remedy for a dismayed individual goes beyond that.

Are you dismayed in that which God called you to do? Your hands have become too weak to act and you have abandoned your God-given task. What you need, my dear friend is revival. Yours is a need beyond strength. You actually need to be made alive once again with respect to your vision.

There's one principal cause of dismay, it seems to me. This is nothing but fear; fear of the uncertain, fear of sacrifice, fear of suffering, fear of the enemy, fear of failing, fear of death etc.

How can you keep yourself from becoming dismayed?

The Bible says, *"See I lay a Stone in Zion, a tested Stone, a precious cornerstone for a sure foundation; the one who trust will never be dismayed."* (Isaiah 28:16).

Nothing drives away fear like trust and God's presence. If you shall trust God for the best, if you shall trust God for the future, if you shall trust Him with your very life, then dismay will never be your portion.

The LORD said to Israel in the midst of all her enemies

> *8* But you, O Israel, my servant,
> Jacob, whom I have chosen,
> you descendants of Abraham my friend,
> *9* I took you from the ends of the earth,
> from its farthest corners I called you.
> I said, "You are my servant;
> I have chosen you and have not rejected you.
> *10* So do not fear, for I am with you;
> do not be dismayed, for I am your God.
> I will strengthen you and help you;
> I will uphold you with my righteous right hand.
> *11* All who rage against you
> will surely be ashamed and disgraced;
> those who oppose you
> will be as nothing and perish.

> *12* Though you search for your enemies,
> you will not find them.
> Those who wage war against you
> will be as nothing at all.
> *13* For I am the Lord, your God,
> who takes hold of your right hand
> and says to you, Do not fear;
> I will help you.
> *14* Do not be afraid, O warm Jacob,
> O little Israel,
> for I myself will help you," declares the Lord,
> your Redeemer, the Holy One of Israel.
> *15* "See, I will make you into a threshing sledge,
> new and sharp, with many teeth.
> You will thresh the mountains and crush them,
> and reduce the hills to chaff.
> *16* You will winnow them, the wind will pick them up,
> and a gale will blow them away.
> But you will rejoice in the Lord
> and glory in the Holy One of Israel."
> (Isaiah 41:8–16)

What you do need is the assurance of His presence. Each time I read these words I am encouraged and trust that what He has promised, the same will He fulfill in my life.

So you need not fear. Why? For He is with you! When? Always, *"even to the end of the age"*.

So you should not be dismayed. Why? Because He is your God. Not some dumb thing but Jehovah Sabbaoth the Lord of the hosts of heaven.

He has promised to strengthen you, to uphold you with His righteous right hand. He has said all who rage against you will surely be ashamed and disgraced. He says those who oppose you will be as nothing and perish. And the list continues.

What drives away fear is not financial security, neither is it material guarantee nor academic qualification but the presence of God. There is no greater assurance than His presence.

Do you still recall what He told the heroes of the faith? To Isaac He said *"Stay in this land for a while, and I will be with you."* (Genesis 26:3)

To Jacob He said *"Go back to the land of your fathers and to your relatives, and I will be with you."* (Genesis 31:3)

Again when Jacob was about to go to Egypt at the invitation of Joseph, the LORD God appeared to him and said:

> *3* "I am God, the God of your father," he said. "Do not be afraid to go down to Egypt, [...] *4* I will go down to Egypt with you [...]"
> (Genesis 46:3-4)

To Moses He said *"I will be with You."* (Exodus 3:12)

To Joshua He said *"As I was with Moses, so I will be with you; I will never leave you nor forsake you."* (Joshua 1:5)

To Gideon He said, *"I will be with you, and you will strike down all the Midianites together"*. (Judges 6:16)

Shall we continue the list? It can go on and on.

To be kept from dismay will need nothing but the assurance of His presence.

Someone might say *"Well I already find myself in a state of dismay, now how do I get out of it?"*

You need His reviving touch.

> Those who dwell under his shadow shall return; they shall be revived like grain, and grow like a vine. Their scent shall be like the wine of Lebanon.
>
> (Hoseah 14:7 NKJV)

Yeah under His shadow, His very presence is the place to return; there you shall be revived. There is no other way to revival than basking in His presence. The cry is to return to the LORD; *"Come let us return to the LORD"*. (Hoseah 6:1a)

After the return what happens?

> *2* After two days he will revive us;
> on the third day he will restore us,
> that we may live in his presence.
> *3* Let us acknowledge the LORD;
> let us press on to acknowledge him.
> As surely as the sun rises,
> he will appear;
> he will come to us like the winter rains,
> like the spring rains that water the earth.
>
> (Hoseah 6:2-3)

There must be a pressing on and surely He will revive you. He will appear as surely as the sun rises.

Get revived!

Reclaim (Redeem)

We said another weapon of the enemy is to produce a di-vision by producing a counterfeit of the original. And most often many vision bearers abandon, ignorantly, the authentic, for pursuit of the fake, in a state of spiritual slumber.

Like the case of the two women cited in 1 Kings 3:16-28 there must be a reclaiming of that which is rightly yours. This can be done only in a revived state – a state of spiritual awareness and alacrity. That's why the last point we just looked at talked of revival, without which it is impossible to reclaim. That woman could not get her real baby – the living one – until she awakened from her slumber. Revival is indispensable for you to be in a position to reclaim your authentic vision. Once there is revival there need to be confrontation, wise confrontation to repossess your vision. The adversary will not give it back to you smiling. He will do everything to let you remain with the dead vision.

> 22 The other woman said, "No! The living one is my son; the dead one is yours."
> But the first one insisted, "No! The dead one is yours; the living one is mine." And so they argued before the king.
> 23 The king said, "This one says, 'My son is alive and your son is dead,' while that one says, 'No! Your son is dead and mine is alive.'"
> (1 Kings 3:22-23)

Take your case to the court of the King of the universe, the Father of all creation. With all wisdom He shall pass the verdict. He can't make mistakes .So you can trust Him. The King you are taking the case to is the One who gave you the vision.

Here there is need for importunity, there is need for persistence in the court of the MOST HIGH, for justice to be done. Do you recall the parable of the persistent widow? (see Luke 18:1-8)

Take your case to the King, the Judge of all the earth and say to Him "Grant me justice against my adversary" and for sure He will see that you get justice and get it speedily. Glory to His Majesty!

Receive

There are some whose visions are irredeemable, for them the devil has succeeded to destroy their vision because actively or passively they took sides with the very enemies – in – disguise to their vision. May be the quest for riches, may be the love of fame, may be the love of money caused them to forfeit their vision in exchange. Every vision forfeited is vision destroyed.

The devil comes to steal, to kill and to destroy. I repeat, many will acknowledge that he has indeed stolen, killed and ultimately destroyed that which was given them by God. The only way out is to receive another vision from God. He is a God of mercy and compassion. A God of another chance. His mercies are new every morning. How great is His faithfulness, to make all things new, to trample our sins and mistakes under foot and treat us from a totally new perspective.

> *1* This is the word that came to Jeremiah from the Lord: *2* "Go down to the potter's house, and there I will give you my message." *3* So I went down to the potter's house, and I saw him working at the wheel. *4* But the pot he was shaping from the clay was marred in his hands; so the

potter formed it into another pot, shaping it as seemed best to him.
5 Then the word of the Lord came to me: *6* "O house of Israel, can I not do with you as this potter does?" declares the Lord. "Like clay in the hand of the potter, so are you in my hand, O house of Israel."
(Jeremiah 18:1-6)

God is not only able but also willing to make the best of you. For Him the future is always brighter as long as, like clay, He has us in His hands. He can always make us into something new. He is the Master Potter.

For those who have never had a vision from God, for His Name, His Kingdom, His will, and those who have had their visions destroyed, we are going to, in the following section, see how to receive a vision from God.

A TWENTY MINUTES STOP

✤ Points to Meditate on

a. *To defeat your enemy, you must recognize him, his weapons and methods and strongholds.*

b. *There are things and habits and even relationships you must renounce so as to come out of distraction.*

c. *The one who recognizes having been displaced or de-positioned has no option but to reposition himself.*

d. *At any given time, all you should present to God is your emptiness, your weariness and weakness for Him to fill.*

e. *Fear, is the principal cause of dismay; fear of the uncertain, fear of sacrifice, fear of suffering, fear of failure etc*

f. *What drives away fear is not financial security, neither is it material guarantee nor academic qualification but the presence of God.*

g. *Revival is indispensable for you if you must reclaim your vision.*

h. *God is not only able but also willing to make the best of you.*

♣ Decisions

....
....
....
....
....
....
....
....
....
....
....
....
....
....
....

♣ Heartcry

"Mighty God, grant me the sprit of discernment to be able to discern the enemies to my vision. Help me act bravely in all that I must renounce so as to stay on focus. I have no strength on my own but emptiness, weariness and weakness. So I come to you to fill and empower me. Make me bold and fearless as I abide in Your presence."

Chapter Seven

THE PATHWAY TO RECEIVING A VISION

There is a passage in the Bible, which will illustrate what I have to say here. It would act as our principal reference, though time and again we shall appeal to other scripture for clarity.

> *35* As Jesus approached Jericho, a blind man was sitting by the roadside begging. *36* When he heard the crowd going by, he asked what was happening. *37* They told him, "Jesus of Nazareth is passing by."
> *38* He called out, "Jesus, Son of David, have mercy on me!"
> *39* Those who led the way rebuked him and told him to be quiet, but he shouted all the more, "Son of David, have mercy on me!"
> *40* Jesus stopped and ordered the man to be brought to him. When he came near, Jesus asked him, *41* "What do you want me to do for you?"
> "Lord, I want to see," he replied.

42 Jesus said to him, "Receive your sight; your faith has healed you."
(Luke 18: 35 – 42)

If there's one need the church has today, it is the need for vision receivers. Many people in the church today have no vision. They are in the church but aren't doing anything year-in – year-out.

When I was younger, very much younger, on public holidays, Sundays and other feasts days, at the entrance of every measure site or city or quarter, I always saw beggars, I mean genuine beggars begging for money. Today is not the case. Not that there are no beggars, but that there are a lot of fake guys out there begging. People who can work have decided to make themselves beggars. Many with great abilities have decided to fake disability and therefore, instead of being the asset they should be to the society have become liabilities. My cry is not about those beggars out there but those in the church who are nothing but liabilities. They never grow because they have no vision.

There are some who must always be prayed for but are not praying for anybody.

There are some who must be encouraged but are not encouraging anybody.

There are some who must be discipled but are discipling nobody.

Some must be given to always, but are giving to nobody.

Others must be led but are leading nobody, not even themselves.

These, I mean, are all people with God given potentials, talents and gifts but are near useless in God's house.

Why? Because of lack of vision.

The blind beggar (Bartimaeus in Marks Gospel) was sitting by the roadside to Jericho. Jericho was a center for business and commerce, a place of action, yet there was someone sitting outside this place of action.

Why? Because Bartimaeus had no vision; he was blinded and veiled to the world around him.

At what roadside are you sitting?

Roadside of spiritual barrenness?

Roadside of spiritual poverty?

Roadside of defeat and failure?

No matter the roadside at which you find yourself, you can come out of that place. How? By receiving a vision. Without vision there can be no action, even if there is it will produce no impact, for impact comes through conviction by the one acting.

There was an open gate to the place of action for Bartimaeus to enter but because of lack of vision, he watched others walking into their destiny while he stayed just where he was.

Are you watching others walking into the place of success while you seem disabled?

Are you watching others walk into the place of financial fulfillment while you sit and watch unable to do a thing?

Are you watching others walking into a life of spiritual fulfillment while you sit and watch unable to get in?

Are you watching others entering a life of emotional fulfillment while you sit and watch things falling apart in your own life?

There's something you can do about it: to receive a vision there must be,

1. Desire

> When he heard the crowd passing by, he asked what was happening. (V 36)

A desire is an earnest wish for something, a longing, a craving or yearning.

Lack of desire, in the church today, for great things is the sole cause of spiritual poverty and bondage. Every great event has always sprung from the simple desire to see something done.

Desire births curiosity. The lack of desire is shown in the fact that too many believers are totally oblivious of their spiritual environment. They don't bother to know what is happening around them or to understand the times.

Bartimaeus was curios and so he asked what was happening in his environment. There is no way you can come out of that visionlessness unless you desire to.

The Pathway to Receiving a Vision

There is no way you can come out of that state of poverty and unrest unless you desire to. Desire is the birthplace of victory. It is the birthplace of discovery which is the pathway to recovery.

Are there some strange things happening in your life or environment? Has your attention been drawn to them or to you they mean nothing?

Bartimaeus inquired of what was happening from someone who could see; someone who had vision. He did not turn to another blind man to ask what was happening. We all need someone, whatever the sphere of our calling, whom we can turn to for explanation for better understanding of our environment, be it in research, business, academics, ministry etc. we must be open to learn from others who have been there before us. Do not surround yourself with people who know what you know and are ignorant of what you are ignorant of, or who have what you have and lack what you lack.

The Bible gives several accounts of mighty things that stemmed out of simple curiosity. We shall look at some.

Rebekah

21 Isaac prayed to the Lord on behalf of his wife, because she was barren. The Lord answered his prayer, and his wife Rebekah became pregnant. *22* The babies jostled each other within her, and she said, "Why is this happening to me?" So she went to inquire of the Lord.
23 The Lord said to her,
"Two nations are in your womb,
and two peoples from within you will be separated;

one people will be stronger than the other,
and the older will serve the younger."
(Genesis 25: 21 – 23)

She noticed something abnormal happening to her. She was curious enough to understand the strange happening in her life.

Are there some strange things happening to you? Get curious about it.

Pharaoh's Daughter

1 Now a man of the house of Levi married a Levite woman, *2* and she became pregnant and gave birth to a son. When she saw that he was a fine child, she hid him for three months. *3* But when she could hide him no longer, she got a papyrus basket for him and coated it with tar and pitch. Then she placed the child in it and put it among the reeds along the bank of the Nile. *4* His sister stood at a distance to see what would happen to him.
5 Then Pharaoh's daughter went down to the Nile to bathe, and her attendants were walking along the river bank. She saw the basket among the reeds and sent her slave girl to get it. *6* She opened it and saw the baby. He was crying, and she felt sorry for him. "This is one of the Hebrew babies," she said.
7 Then his sister asked Pharaoh's daughter, "Shall I go and get one of the Hebrew women to nurse the baby for you?"
8 "Yes, go," she answered. And the girl went and got the baby's mother. *9* Pharaoh's daughter said to her, "Take this baby and nurse him for me, and I will pay you." So the woman took the baby and nursed him. *10* When the child grew older, she took him to Pharaoh's daughter and

he became her son. She named him Moses, saying, "I drew him out of the water."
(Exodus 2:1-10)

She noticed a basket among the reeds and desired to know what this meant. She was curious enough to find out what was in that basket, and why a basket among reeds.

Moses

1 Now Moses was tending the flock of Jethro his father-in-law, the priest of Midian, and he led the flock to the far side of the desert and came to Horeb, the mountain of God. *2* There the angel of the Lord appeared to him in flames of fire from within a bush. Moses saw that though the bush was on fire it did not burn up. *3* So Moses thought, "I will go over and see this strange sight–why the bush does not burn up."
4 When the Lord saw that he had gone over to look, God called to him from within the bush, "Moses! Moses!" And Moses said, "Here I am."
5 "Do not come any closer," God said. "Take off your sandals, for the place where you are standing is holy ground."
6 Then he said, "I am the God of your father, the God of Abraham, the God of Isaac and the God of Jacob." At this, Moses hid his face, because he was afraid to look at God.
(Exodus 3:1-6)

Moses saw this strange sight and was curious enough to go closer and know why the bush was in flames and was not burnt up. He responded to the strange happening in his environment.

There was a desire to understand the mystery of the unconsumed burning bush.

David

David had a desire, not because of some external happenings but that which stemmed from his heart in trying to do something for his God.

> *1* After the king was settled in his palace and the Lord had given him rest from all his enemies around him, *2* he said to Nathan the prophet, "Here I am, living in a palace of cedar, while the ark of God remains in a tent."
> *3* Nathan replied to the king, "Whatever you have in mind, go ahead and do it, for the Lord is with you."
> (2 Samuel 7:1-3)

His desire was to build a house for his God. He wanted to do something great for his God.

Let desire give birth to curiosity in each of us, do not become like Balaam to whom nothing was strange, not even the speech of a donkey.

2. Decision

Desire prepares you for action, but decision sets you to action.

There're people with lots of desire in their heart, but over the years it has remained just a desire. Decision is that which translates desire to action.

He called out, *"Jesus son of David, have mercy on me!"*

The Pathway to Receiving a Vision

Every desire not translated into a decision becomes abortive. Bartimaeus' desire, through curiosity, led to a decision to shout. As you come to the point of decision, know that your decision will:

I Encounter a Reaction

Once Bartimaeus decided and shouted, he met a violent reaction from those around, who told him to be quiet. Every decision will meet opposition. Until Bartimaeus shouted nobody bothered if he existed, no one took note of him but once he shouted, once he made a decision he encountered a reaction from without. Expect those who have not bothered about you until now to oppose you once you decide to have things changed in your life. Once you take the decision you must take, expect the devil to marshal his forces against you. We have just said decision sets you to action. Let me give you a bit of physics here; Newton's third law states that *"for every action there is an equal but opposite reaction"*. So if your decision sets you to action expect an equal but opposing reaction from your environment.

II Lead to Revelation

For Rebekah, once she desired to know what was happening, there was the decision to go and inquire of the LORD. For her it did not end at the level of wishful thinking, there was a decision to get out of the normal routine of her life so as to go inquire of the LORD. The result is very encouraging. Her decision brought about a great revelation from God that is determining the course of events even today.

Do you need a vision? Seek a revelation from God and decide to inquire of Him.

III Demand Responsibility

For pharaoh's daughter, her desire to know what was in the basket meant her taking the decision to send someone to get the basket from among the reeds.

Seeing what was in the basket moved her heart, a crying helpless baby, and this led to compassion – love and mercy in action.

For too many of us, the cries of the suffering, sick, and dying people all around us have meant nothing because of lack of decision. Many times we seem to wish we were helping but fail to decide to help. We refuse to take decisions because we are afraid of responsibility. There are many things in God's household we can each be involved in but we have not decided to because we do not want to be responsible for them.

For pharaoh's daughter, it was a responsibility of looking for a nanny for this little child. It meant her being financially responsible for the child.

Are you afraid of responsibility? If so there can be no vision for you. Vision means responsibility.

For all the people God has ever called, they always did have a responsibility, no matter how mean it seemed.

- ○ Moses was a shepherd when he was called. (Exodus 3:1-2)
- ○ Gideon was busy, threshing wheat. (Judges 3:10-12)

- Amos, shepherd a flock and also took care of fig trees. (Amos 7:14)
- Elisha was plowing a field when he was called. (1 Kings 19:19)
- Peter, Andrew, James and John were fishing when they were called. (Matthew 4:18-22).
- Matthew was in his tax collector's booth when he was called. (Matthew 9:9)

You must decide to bear a responsibility in God's house if you must have a vision.

IV Mean Taking a Risk

Pharaoh's daughter took the decision to get the basket, not knowing what was inside. Nowadays it could mean a time bomb or some other explosive. Her decision to get it meant her taking a risk.

Moses took the decision to get closer to the flame. For him it could mean being consumed by the flames, but however, he decided to move towards it.

Decision, for you too, will mean taking a risk. For too many of us, we've been too long in our comfort zones, where safety is kind of guaranteed and so there is no vision for us. It may mean risking your finances, it may mean *"risking your future"*, it may mean risking your relationships and it may mean risking your own very life. But risk is inevitable.

Nehemiah took the risk of demanding the king's help. (Nehemiah 2:1-3)

Esther took the risk of going into the king's presence without invitation. (Esther 4:15-16)

Risk is inevitable for the one who must receive a vision. Are you willing to risk it for Jesus?

V   Finally, Decision Can Meet Refusal

It is but true that it is not all a man desires or decides to do which God endorses. At times decision is met with refusal from God. In the case of David, God did not allow him to build the Temple for Him. However, God still gave him the opportunity to be a great part of the Temple by providing almost all that was needed. Though it is known as Solomon's temple, the design and material for it was all David's. At least he received the design from God. Though God may not allow you to be the principal actor of that which is in your heart to do, He will allow you to be a great part of it, even from the background.

3. Determination

> Those who led the way rebuked him and told him to be quiet, but he shouted all the more, "Son of David, have mercy on me!"

By determination here I mean the exercise of decisive force or power.

Decision is what will set you to action but determination is what keeps you in action. Every decision is met with obstacles and only determination, that firm resolve, would lead you to overcome those obstacles.

If there is one thing you should know, it is that not everyone around you wants your progress. Not all will be happy to see you change states. Like Bartimaeus you are surely going to face opposition. You'll meet discouraging comments and attitudes. Do not expect to be applauded because you now seek a vision. You need to resolve to have it at all cost. The sad thing here is that Bartimaeus' decision to get his vision was opposed by *"those who led the way"*.

The very people who were to guide him in this path to receiving his vision and fulfill his destiny turned to oppose him. Is that not what we find in the world today? Those who seem to be ahead trying to prevent others from fulfilling their destinies? We see it everywhere, in business, in research and worst of all in ministry.

God requires something beyond just a decision. He wants to see a determination in each one of us. Let's revisit the Book, for an illustrative account.

> **8** Then Naomi said to her two daughters-in-law, "Go back, each of you, to your mother's home. May the Lord show kindness to you, as you have shown to your dead and to me. **9** May the Lord grant that each of you will find rest in the home of another husband."
> Then she kissed them and they wept aloud **10** and said to her, "We will go back with you to your people."
> **11** But Naomi said, "Return home, my daughters. Why would you come with me? Am I going to have any more sons, who could become your husbands? **12** Return home, my daughters; I am too old to have another husband. Even if I thought there was still hope for me–even if I had a husband tonight and then gave birth to sons– **13** would

you wait until they grew up? Would you remain unmarried for them? No, my daughters. It is more bitter for me than for you, because the Lord's hand has gone out against me!"

14 At this they wept again. Then Orpah kissed her mother-in-law good-by, but Ruth clung to her.

15 "Look,'" said Naomi, "your sister-in-law is going back to her people and her gods. Go back with her."

16 But Ruth replied, "Don't urge me to leave you or to turn back from you. Where you go I will go, and where you stay I will stay. Your people will be my people and your God my God. *17* Where you die I will die, and there I will be buried. May the Lord deal with me, be it ever so severely, if anything but death separates you and me."

18 When Naomi realized that Ruth was determined to go with her, she stopped urging her.

19 So the two women went on until they came to Bethlehem. When they arrived in Bethlehem, the whole town was stirred because of them, and the women exclaimed, "Can this be Naomi?"

(Ruth 1:8-19)

Here, I am not interested just in the narrative, it is indeed a sad narrative. What interests me are the implications, the lessons that can be drawn from the narrative.

Here both Orpah and Ruth decided to return to Bethlehem with their mother-in-law (Verses 7 and 10) and they both met with a refusal – a persistent one from her, to return to Bethlehem. Now I want you to realize what kept Ruth along that path to Bethlehem – the house of bread, while Orpah decided to withdraw from the road to the ' house of bread':

"When Naomi realized that Ruth was determined to go with her, she stopped urging her". The only reason is determination. Determination is that which brings a breakthrough against every external obstacle.

There are a number of things I'll like you to see from the passage above, the Implications of determination.

I   Determination Implies a Cross

Ruth was willing to carry her cross of remaining a widow the rest of her life. Naomi couldn't dissuade her from coming along by the fact that she could not bring forth a son who could become Ruth's husband (Verse11). In other words she decided to carry her cross of widowhood.

Determination for you too, will imply a cross, cross of shame, mockery and despise. However determination leads you to carry it daily and follow the Master wherever He may lead. For her it meant no security for the future neither of a husband nor a son. (Verses 12 and 13)

Orpah turned back from the road to the house of bread because she wouldn't carry her cross of widowhood.

II   Determination Requires Conviction

"Look," Naomi said, "Your sister-in-law is going back to her people and her gods. Go back with her". (Verse 15)

If Ruth had no conviction from within, if all she relied on was some external support, if all she relied on was positive circumstances she would obviously havé returned. But Ruth had a conviction on which her determination could stand.

Determination can never stand on popular opinion or external evidences, for it will soon come crumbling.

Do you have personal conviction about what you feel God is leading you to? It is indispensable. You can't go far without it. You won't strive for long without it.

III Determination Requires Commitment

> Don't urge me to leave you or to turn back from you. Where you go I will go, where you stay I will stay.
> (Verse 16a and b)

Is there a greater way to have expressed her heart's commitment to Naomi? Ruth was determined to go with Naomi and this for her meant a commitment. You must be committed to whatever you want for determination to carry you along. Ruth was committed to Naomi's leadership. Each of us must be committed to the Spirit's leadership, wherever and however He may lead us. Engage and pledge yourself to His Cause, His Name, His glory.

To what and to whom are you committed?

IV Determination Requires Courage

Courage is that quality of mind, which meets danger or opposition with intrepidity, calmness, and firmness. It is that quality of being fearless.

"Your people will be my people and your God my God." (Verse 16c). It is certain that Ruth was not ignorant of who Naomi's people were, nor who her God was. She knew for sure that the Jewish race was the most hated, despised and attacked by

the surrounding nations. She knew Israel had just suffered a severe famine. She knew the consequences of identifying with Naomi's people. Nothing but courage caused her to make this pledging identification. What if Naomi's people were not welcoming? What if they were hostile? What if they rejected her? What if Naomi's God demanded her (Ruth's) life? There was a lot of uncertainty and only courage on the part of Ruth could push her to be willing to face these unknowns.

She knew she was going from her family, her own people, her own land to a people she had never known, to a land she had never been to, to worship a God she knew nothing about. What courage!

Is there any doubt she became what she became in Israel?

V Determination Implies Consecration

To consecrate means to dedicate solemnly, as from emotions of gratitude or convictions of duty.

> Where you die I will die, and there I will be buried. May the LORD deal with me, be it ever so severely, if anything but death separates you and me.

This was an irrevocable laying down of her life on the altar of Naomi. God is looking for boys and girls, men and women with the heart of Ruth to impart to them His vision. People who are sure to say *"nothing but death will separate me from the vision God gives me!"* Men and women willing to lay down their lives for the sake of the call. Will you not lay it down, irrevocably? Will you not give Him your all? It demands your separation from the common, wholly and completely giving up your life to the call.

Determination implies consecration, nothing short of that; if not it will amount to nothing. If your determination does not push you to wholly give yourself to Him, like a living sacrifice, then it is carnal determination, which is of the flesh and will soon end in the flesh.

Do you know that the very first time Bartimaeus cried out, Jesus heard him? Why did the Lord not stop immediately? Why did He act as though He cared less? So that Bartimaeus could have the opportunity to express his determination.

4. Desperation

Desperation is energized despair, vigorous in action, reckless of consequences.

In the account of Bartimaeus in Mark's gospel, I have a particular interest in Mark 10:50.

After Bartimaeus had gotten the Lord's attention, there was an open door in front of him with an invitation to come in. He had succeeded in having his breakthrough against all external obstacles.

While determination leads to the overcoming of external obstacles and opposition, it is desperation which will lead to the overcoming of personal barriers and hindrances.

> Throwing his cloak aside, he jumped to his feet and came to Jesus.
> (Mark 10: 50)

Bartimaeus did not care about the cost of his cloak, it did not bother him how long it took him to save for the cloak. Can you imagine a beggar throwing away his cloak? May be it was all he had as shield from the sun or cold. It was surely dear to him but he however had to throw it away. Why? Because he knew it was going to be a hindrance if he had to cheer up and run through that open door to receive his sight. Bartimaeus had to do away with his old identity of the cloak of blindness. He had to do away with the security he found by wearing the cloak of blindness that licensed him to beg. Desperation is what is needed to shake you from every sense of false security to the pursuit of what God has in store for you. Many are trying to run with their cloaks on–too many, though cherished, but unnecessary things which though innocent in themselves will hinder that upward call. In a state of desperation you and I can sacrifice that which is so dear to us and that is just the need of many today.

It is sad that too many have come close to receiving but because of self-indulgence, they have failed to.

Are you desperate for a vision? Or you are still at the level of desire. You must get to the level of desperation.

Desperation, too, has its own implications.

I Separation

Bartimaeus had to separate himself from his cloak so as to run freely to receive his vision. He had to separate from his old identity of a beggarly lifestyle; he had to do away with his license to beg. He carried out a clear separation. There are things in your life from which you must separate so as to receive your vision.

II Surrendering

Because Bartimaeus was desperate, he surrendered his right to keep his cloak. Here is another narrative to drive home our point:

> *3* Now there were four men with leprosy at the entrance of the city gate. They said to each other, "Why stay here until we die? *4* If we say, 'We'll go into the city'—the famine is there, and we will die. And if we stay here, we will die. So let's go over to the camp of the Arameans and surrender. If they spare us, we live; if they kill us, then we die."
> (2 Kings 7:3-4)

These blind men in state of physical hunger and starvation found themselves in a tight corner; rejection on one side and the threat of death on the other. They were at the point were they just had to do something. It was all left to them.

"Let's go over to the camp of the Arameans and surrender" was their resolution. Their desperation led them to surrender their right to live. *"If they spare us, we live; if they kill us, then we die".*

Have you reached that state in your longing for a God-given vision? If not, you are not very prepared for it.

III Supplication

> *1* After this, the Moabites and Ammonites with some of the Meunites came to make war on Jehoshaphat.

2 Some men came and told Jehoshaphat, "A vast army is coming against you from Edom, from the other side of the Sea. It is already in Hazazon Tamar" (that is, En Gedi). *3* Alarmed, Jehoshaphat resolved to inquire of the Lord, and he proclaimed a fast for all Judah. *4* The people of Judah came together to seek help from the Lord; indeed, they came from every town in Judah to seek him.
(2 Chronicles 20:1-4)

9 Jabez was more honorable than his brothers. His mother had named him Jabez, saying, "I gave birth to him in pain." *10* Jabez cried out to the God of Israel, "Oh, that you would bless me and enlarge my territory! Let your hand be with me, and keep me from harm so that I will be free from pain." And God granted his request.
(1 Chronicles 4:9-10)

Desperate Jabez and desperate Jehoshaphat were at a point where all was beyond their power. You and I too need to reach such a point, where we indeed know that all is beyond our human capabilities and abilities. This shall push us to the art of supplication, crying out to God, proclaiming a fast to seek the help of the Almighty.

IV Sacrifice

Bartimaeus did sacrifice his cloak for his sight. This is where desperation will push you to, a totally new and different plain of living, that of sacrifice, where all else will be laid on the altar of your call or vision. Desperation will ultimately lead to sacrifice. There once was a king in a midst of battle and on the verge of defeat. The Bible says,

> Then he took his firstborn son, who was to succeed him as king, and offered him as a sacrifice on the city wall. The fury against Israel was great; they withdrew and returned to their own land.
>
> (2 Kings 3:27)

Here is a king who was on the verge of defeat and conquest. He was about losing the sovereignty and independence of his kingdom. Many of his people had been slaughtered, his towns destroyed, his sources of water blocked, trees cut down. Only one town was left; where the king was and this too came under attack.

The king was in a tight corner – a desperate man. What did he do? He resolved to sacrifice his successor. Desperation, led to sacrifice and sacrifice turned over the tides, and the Bible says, *"The fury against Israel was great"*.

That is what sacrifice does, painful sacrifice. What prayers and supplication cannot do, sacrifice will.

> *Are you ready for sacrifice? It may be your job, it may be your education, it may be some hours of sleep, it may be some comfort, it may be some more hours of hard work, and it may be financial security. Sacrifice will mean different things for different people. But the underlying denominator is that sacrifice causes pain and discomfort. it brings a certain degree of loss to the one who offers it. Whatever it means for you, are you ready?*

Some facts about determination and desperation

- Determination creates the open door; desperation gets you to walk through that open door.

- Determination gets God's attention; desperation gets what you need.
- Determination lets God say *"Call him"*; desperation leads Him to ask *"What is it you want"*.
- Determination leads you to overcome external obstacles; desperation sets you free from self-indulgence.
- Determination can mean careful persistence; desperation means reckless persistence.
- A man who is determined can get desperate; a desperate man has reached the end of himself.
- Determination can end at the level of the will; desperation gets to the emotions.
- A man can be determined inwardly, without outward expression; a man can never be desperate without being seen externally.
- Determination says I should; desperation says I must.

V Delight

Delight in something talks of great pleasure and joyful satisfaction with the thing in question.

This must be there when you must have received your vision in order to get all on the rails.

Of Bartimaeus it is said:

> Immediately he received his sight and followed Jesus, praising God. (Luke 18:43a)

He followed Jesus and praised God. This expresses nothing but delight in that which God had given him. A man praises what he delights in; a man follows what he delights in.

If the vision of God given you must grow, you'll have to delight in it. Why? Because:

VI Delight Implies Concentration

To concentrate means to focus your attention upon a single object, problem or task.

For results you must concentrate on your God – given vision, even at the price of all else. It's worth it. You have to focus your attention and resources in that God – given task.

VII Delight Implies Cherishing

When a man cherishes something, he holds it as dear to him; he treats it as dear to him. He protects it from anything which may harm it. He nourishes and nurtures it until it gets to full maturity.

You nourish and nurture the vision by thinking constantly of it, by praying for it, by relating with people who can teach you and help your vision to grow, making use of every opportunity to learn.

You protect it by being watchful and guarding against distraction and discouragement. It will demand spending much time in God's presence, building confidence and hope. This will lead you to esteem it as priceless, and every other thing will fade in the light of what God has called you to do.

Hallelujah!

A THIRTY MINUTES STOP

✣ **Points to Meditate on**

a. *If there's one need in the church today, it is the need for vision receivers.*

b. *The lack of desire for great things is shown in the fact that too many people are totally oblivious of their spiritual environment.*

c. *Every desire not quickly transformed into decision becomes abortive.*

d. *If you must make a decision, you must be willing to go out of your comfort zone where safety is guaranteed.*

e. *Decision is what sets you to action but determination is what keeps you in action.*

f. *To stay determined, you must be willing to carry your cross, which may mean shame and aloneness, mockery and rejection.*

g. *Determination never stands on popular opinion or external evidences but on inner convictions.*

h. *God is looking for men and women, boys and girls who are willing to say "nothing but death will separate me from the vision God gives me".*

i. *Whereas determination leads you to overcome external obstacles, desperation leads you to overcome personal barriers and self-indulgence.*
j. *You need to arrive at a point where you indeed see that all is beyond your power and human capacities and capabilities.*
k. *You nourish and nurture your vision by thinking of it constantly, praying for it and relating to people who can teach you and help your vision to grow.*

✤ Decisions

✣ Heartcry

"Father, I want to be ever sensitive to and conscious of my spiritual environment; I want to translate my desires to decision and get out of my comfort zone into the place of action. Lord, I am ready to carry my cross and hold to my cause even when I am the only one on that road. Lead me to those I can learn from. I pray for a teachable heart, willing to learn new things."

HOW TO ACCOMPLISH YOUR VISION

After having received a vision, the next step is getting to accomplish that vision. There are essential ingredients to accomplishing any vision irrespective of the size and interval during which it must be accomplished.

Paul said *"Tell Archippus: 'See to it that you complete the work you have received in the Lord.'"* (Colossians 4:17). His advice to Archippus was to accomplish his vision. It does not suffice to receive a vision, what matters is the accomplishment of the vision.

28 Suppose one of you wants to build a tower. Will he not first sit down and estimate the cost to see if he has enough money to complete it? *29* For if he lays the foundation and is not able to finish it, everyone who sees it will ridicule him, *30* saying, "This fellow began to build and was not able to finish."

(Luke 14:28-30)

1. Count the Cost

After a man or woman has received a vision, it is paramount to count the cost of accomplishing such a vision. In the light of God's presence questions like:

I. What will it take with respect to natural and spiritual gifts for this vision to be accomplished?
II. What will it take in the domain of manpower for the realization of this vision?
III. What kind of material resources do I need to accomplish my vision?
IV. What are the financial implications in accomplishing my vision?
V. What difficulties am I likely to encounter in trying to accomplish my vision?
VI. Am I willing to pursue this vision right to the end come what may?

Such questions will help bring you in confrontation with the reality; the reality of your incapacity to accomplish anything without God, the reality of depending upon God alone for the accomplishment of a vision no matter how small it may appear.

You've got to count the cost, prayerfully count the cost.

2. Consider (Evaluate) your Resources

After counting the cost, the next step is to evaluate the resources available, honestly, in the light of God's presence. Questions like the following will help.

I. Do I have the natural and spiritual gifts needed for such a calling?
II. Do I have the manpower needed for the realization of my vision?
III. Do I have available the material resources needed to accomplish such a vision?
IV. How can I get the finances needed?
V. How do I face the difficulties that may be involved?

Such questions, again I say, are to bring you to a point of seeing that, God does not call us to do the things we are able to do because of what we have or who we are without Him. They are meant to bring us to a point where, faced with such challenges, like Paul, are able to say *"My God will supply all my needs according to His glorious riches in Christ Jesus"*.

3. Carve out a Plan

"But the noble man makes noble plans, and by noble deeds he stands" (Isaiah 32:8).

God does not forbid us from making plans. As noble people He expects us to make noble plans. That's why He commands us to *"think of things that are noble"*. As we think of noble things, we conceive noble ideas that lead us to noble plans.

God's problem is when plans are hidden from Him; when plans are made and executed without seeking His counsel (See Isaiah 25:15).

He will happily visa every plan made in accordance with His will as we see in Proverbs 16:3 – *"Commit to the Lord whatever you do and your plans will succeed."* and He will readily disqualify any plan which is not in accordance with His will (Isaiah 30:1-5).

In James 4:13-15, the problem is not the plan-making but plan-execution without the approval of the Almighty God. Without noble plans, there can be no noble deeds. Such a plan must consist of both short and medium term visions, which can be checked and evaluated as time passes. It must involve how to get the necessary resources for the accomplishment of your vision.

4. Communicate your Vision.

To better put across this point, I will like us to take a case-study:

> *1* Now the whole world had one language and a common speech. *2* As men moved eastward, they found a plain in Shinar and settled there.
> *3* They said to each other, "Come, let's make bricks and bake them thoroughly." They used brick instead of stone, and tar for mortar. *4* Then they said, "Come, let us build ourselves a city, with a tower that reaches to the heavens, so that we may make a name for ourselves and not be scattered over the face of the whole earth."

5 But the Lord came down to see the city and the tower that the men were building. *6* The Lord said, "If as one people speaking the same language they have begun to do this, then nothing they plan to do will be impossible for them. *7* Come, let us go down and confuse their language so they will not understand each other."
8 So the Lord scattered them from there over all the earth, and they stopped building the city. *9* That is why it was called Babel– because there the Lord confused the language of the whole world. From there the Lord scattered them over the face of the whole earth.
(Genesis 11:1-9)

These guys came together and evaluated what was needed to accomplish their vision. They ensured that the resources were available before they set out to commence construction (V3).

Our focus here is the sixth verse.

The strength of mankind lies in the power of effective communication.

At the beginning they had communicated the vision to each other and nothing could stop them.

From what the LORD said here, the greatest cause of failure and defeat is lack of understanding. This stems from ineffective communication between any two persons or groups of people. Ineffective communication sets the stage for confusion and eventual defeat. Anything that hinders effective communication is fuel for confusion. This includes,

- Suspicion
- Duplicity

- Despise
- Ingratitude
- Superiority
- Inferiority
- Competition
- Cynicism
- Criticism

The result of breaking the people's capacity to communicate with each other was that they all scattered. In the whole Bible there are just two instances where a *"congregation"* scattered.

- Where there is no effective communication as seen in Genesis 11:8 and
- Where there is no leadership (Matthew 26:61).

The implication of this is that a leader who does not effectively communicate his vision cannot build a victorious and invincible people, no matter how much allegiance they pledge. You should measure your leadership by your capacity to effectively communicate with the people you are leading.

The Lord Jesus communicated His vision to His disciples and made it possible for there to be effective communication between His sheep and Him even after He was gone.

> *12* I have much more to say to you, more than you can now bear. *13* But when he, the Spirit of truth, comes, he will guide you into all truth. He will not speak on his own; he will speak only what he hears, and he will tell you what is yet to come. *14* He will bring glory to me by taking from what is mine and making it known to you. *15* All that belongs to the Father is mine. That is why I

said the Spirit will take from what is mine and make it known to you.
(John 16:12-15).

To accomplish your vision you must communicate it.

5. Cooperate with Others

Surely someone was asking; *"What is the purpose of communication and to whom do I communicate my vision?"*

Well, the purpose of communication is to enhance co-operation. No one is complete in himself. The questions you asked yourself at the beginning surely brought you to a point where you saw the need for God and for others. For our Lord, it was a group of twelve whom He selected to influence a large group of seventy-two.

We must ask the Spirit's guidance in selecting the people to whom to communicate the vision. He alone knows what we need and who is able to compliment you in areas of weakness. Communication is the bridge between every vision and the necessary cooperation for accomplishment. There can be no co-operation without mutual understanding and there can be no understanding without communication. Those with whom you co-operate are the partners in your vision, who should stand with you in providing the necessary resources from spiritual, through human to material and financial. Know that you don't have everything and you can't do everything. Ask the Lord to bring you those with whom you must co-operate. They surely will come from different walks of life and backgrounds. The essential thing is the common vision, which has brought you together.

The Lord said in Genesis 11:6, that for any group of people who:

1. Have a vision;
2. Communicate effectively (speak one language);
3. Co-operate with each other.

Nothing will be impossible for them. in fact impossibility will be erased from their vocabulary. This is the testimony of the omniscient God.

6. Celebrate your Co-workers

When you celebrate those who work with you, their input and output will increase; they in turn will celebrate you and increase your own input and output.

When you apply these nuggets, nothing will be impossible for you to do.

Inspiration from David

There're a number of points I'd want us to draw from the mighty man, David's instructions to His son Solomon respecting the temple he had to build.

> *9* "And you, my son Solomon, acknowledge the God of your father, and serve him with wholehearted devotion and with a willing mind, for the Lord searches every heart and understands every motive behind the thoughts. If

you seek him, he will be found by you; but if you forsake him, he will reject you forever. *10* Consider now, for the Lord has chosen you to build a temple as a sanctuary. Be strong and do the work."
(1 Chronicles 28:9-10)

The points we draw from here are points that are also essential to accomplish any vision but are interwoven in the six points given above.

1. Acknowledging the Lord

This talks of the Lordship of the Lord over one's life. Submitting to His rule over your life, to His will for each stage of your vision. His methods and workings in your life are imperative to realize your vision. You must be committed not to your own instincts but to His leading and direction. You must acknowledge Him, not in words only but in attitude and action.

2. Serve the Lord with a Wholehearted Devotion

Fickle heartedness will take you nowhere. Serving the Lord with dividedness of heart brings you no reward. If you must work, you must work with your whole heart.

3. Serve the Lord with a Willing Mind

There must be a willingness in the mind to do what God has asked you to do. It does not please God when we do things as under compulsion. He desires a willingness of both the heart and the mind.

4. Seek the Lord for Details

There must be asking and receiving of direction and directives from the Lord. Unless this happens there can be no accomplishment of a vision. David sought the Lord and He granted to David two things concerning the temple; *"All this,"* David said, *"I have in writing from the hand of the LORD upon me, and he gave me understanding in all the details of the plan."* (1 Chronicles 28:19)

1. Details of all that the temple was to consist of, and
2. Understanding of the whole plan of the temple.

This was done by impressing the plan upon David's spirit. At every one moment you must be open enough to receive that which He drops into your spirit. Most often the fine details will come in this manner. Seek spiritual wisdom and understanding from the Lord. (See Colossians 1: 9-12).

5. Work Hard

Finally, you must work hard and exercise self-discipline and determination to accomplishment your vision.

> Whatever your hand finds to do, do it with all your might, for in the grave, where you are going, there is neither working nor planning nor knowledge nor wisdom.
> (Ecclesiastes 9:10)

God has given you work to do, see to it that you complete the work. God has chosen you to do a work for Him; you must be careful; you must be strong and do the work. Remember you are not indispensable; the Lord can put you aside. Heed to David's warning to Solomon. As long as you are committed to and working hard in your vision you always have the Lord's backing.

A TEN-MINUTES STOP

✤ **Points to Ponder**

a. *It does not suffice to receive a vision, what matters is accomplishing the vision.*

b. *You need to make noble plans for you to do noble deeds. Such plans must consist of both long and short term tasks.*

c. *Measure your leadership by your capacity to effectively communicate with those you are leading.*

d. *Know that you don't have and you can't do everything.*

e. *As long as you are committed to and work hard in your vision you always have the Lord's backing.*

✤ **Decision**

....
....
....
....
....
....
....

✤ Heartcry

"Lord, I acknowledge that I do not have all that it takes; I need others, I need You. Help me to make noble plans in accordance with Your will. Help me to communicate effectively with the partners to my vision so as to realize the necessary results"

How to Accomplish your Vision – 2

In His Presence

We have talked about God's presence as all that a man needs to set out into that which God has called him to do. We talked of *"with"* His presence. Here I want us to talk about the power of staying in His presence.

> The men turned away and went toward Sodom, but Abraham remained standing before the LORD."
> (Genesis 18:22)

If you must fulfill your destiny, the presence of God must be your home. God's presence must be home for you if you must succeed. Neglecting the presence of God is neglecting the very path to success.

- Revelations come in His presence.
- Empowerment takes place in His presence.
- Anointing takes place in His presence.

For how long can you tarry in His presence?

- Remaining in His presence emboldens and encourages.
- Standing before God gives Him opportunity to show you who you are and what you are.
- Standing before God must become a normal way of life for the one who must fulfill his destiny.
- Remaining in the presence of God is giving Him time to work in you; it enables you to develop your vision to maturity.
- A listening ear and heart can only be developed in His presence.
- In His presence you shall develop the attitude of positive approach to situations, knowing with God all things are possible.
- Staying in His presence enables you to know Him personally.

Three years ago while I meditated on John 20:1,10-16, the Lord spoke to me and I wrote down the following:

> *Tarry alone in My presence with the determination to see Me, to hear Me and to find Me. Tarry alone in My presence, tarry around the grave where I was buried, you shall discover My resurrection when others have gone back home. Tarry and linger in earnestness to see Me when others have gone home. I shall call you by name and show Myself to you. I shall open your eyes to behold your resurrected Lord.*

You seem to always come and go back home. No! Tarry away from home- your usual comfort, ease, eating habits and from your usual company, and linger in the dark and cold and I'll show My self to you. Then you shall never return home but will go from home to proclaim my resurrection and truly you shall become a witness for Me to all around.

It meant for Mary loneliness around the grave, it meant for her cold in the dark, it meant for her tears and weeping. It shall mean no less for you.

So we see that continuous withdrawal into His presence is indispensable for the fulfillment of your destiny. Every vision has as birthplace the presence of God. Unless a vision is born in God's presence nurtured in God's presence and accomplished first in prayer before the Lord, such a vision cannot be realized.

The success or failure of a vision can be known from its birthplace. The first signs of failure are at the place of prayer because failing at the place of prayer is failing everywhere. Failing to pray is praying to fail.

Every phase of your vision must be prayed through. Standing before the LORD is waiting on God; it is being at God's disposal waiting for instruction to execute.

Abraham remained standing before the LORD

This signifies nothing but intercession, establishing revelations received through prayer.

Your success lies in God's presence. It incubates the vision, empowers the vision bearer and propels him into the future.

Standing before God gives you authority to speak to situations and have them obey.

The extent of your power and authority lies in how much of God's presence you are carrying.

At the Foot of the Cross

25 Near the cross of Jesus stood his mother, his mother's sister, Mary the wife of Clopas, and Mary Magdalene. *26* When Jesus saw his mother there, and the disciple whom he loved standing nearby, he said to his mother, "Dear woman, here is your son," *27* and to the disciple, "Here is your mother." From that time on, this disciple took her into his home.
(John 19:25-27)

It is a blessing to stay near the cross, beholding and contemplating the price paid, by the beloved Savior, for your sins. In the sight of the cross all else loses it's value and the purpose of the cross first for your own life, then for the whole world will stand.

Near His cross the Lord takes care of your needs before you know. Those who stay near the cross have their needs at the center of the Lord's mind.

It is near the cross that the Lord assigns us. Near the cross the Lord shows us His needs and those of others and assigns us as His co-workers to meet those needs. As He assigns us to meet the needs of others, He assigns others to meet our own needs. In the family of Jesus responsibilities are received nowhere else but at the foot of the cross on which He died. The more a life portrays the cross of Christ the greater the responsibility that will be given.

- No cross no responsibility.
- Little cross little responsibility.
- More cross more responsibility.

If the vision must grow in the Holy Spirit power, the cross life is a must. Move closer to the cross, the place of suffering, closer to the place of pain. The cross is the centrality of God's will and purpose for mankind. The cross is the place of deliverance, the place of laying down of burdens, the place of abandonment of the love of the world and all that impairs a vision.

Here is a poem for you:

> Let pain and suffering multiply
> So more on You I will rely.
> The world, its wooing, Lord crucify
> So all to me I will count but loss
> And lay my all at the foot of the cross

> Oh! That there is no further delay
> Even just for one more day
> There may be a greater price to pay.
> Now all to you count but loss
> And lay your all at the foot of the cross.

> Come nearer My cross and stay
> Away from it you are sure to stray
> Apart from it there's no other way
> All to you must be counted loss
> And lay your all at the foot of the cross.

Put an end to all selfish dreams
And let the flow of My living streams
O come and have a taste of My cream
Then all to you will be counted loss
And abandoned at the foot of the cross.

Bring all your struggles to an end
And give Me your heart to mend
So the heavens for you I can rend
And to you my every blessing send
When you lay all at the foot of the cross.

E.C.Nakeli
08/07/02

As you stay near the cross, His Words in Genesis 18:14 and Jeremiah 32:27 become life to you. In a new way you'll discover that nothing is too hard for God to do. No miracle is too hard for God to perform. No breakthrough too hard for God to bring out. Just nothing is too hard for the Almighty God. No calling too hard for God to enable you to fulfill. No vision too great to be accomplished through God.

When all evidences are gone, nothing is too hard for God.

When all possibilities seem closed, nothing is too hard for God.

When all hope is gone, nothing is too hard for God to do.

When your faith has failed you, nothing is too hard for God to do.

When the mountains on the way to your destiny seem too big, nothing is too hard for God to do.

When the river you need to cross to the land of your destiny seems to have overflowed its banks nothing is too hard for God to do.

When your Red Sea seems too wide, nothing is too hard for God to do. Praise His Holy Name!

Your Purpose Determines a lot

16 When the men got up to leave, they looked down toward Sodom, and Abraham walked along with them to see them on their way. 17 Then the Lord said, "Shall I hide from Abraham what I am about to do? 18 Abraham will surely become a great and powerful nation, and all nations on earth will be blessed through him. 19 For I have chosen him, so that he will direct his children and his household after him to keep the way of the Lord by doing what is right and just, so that the Lord will bring about for Abraham what he has promised him."

(Genesis 18:16-19)

The dealings of God with Abraham were determined by His purpose for Abraham.

1. Abraham's blessing was determined by His purpose or calling.

To fulfill your destiny, you need not envy another man's blessing because no two people have the same purpose. Your blessing does not determine your calling but your calling determines your blessing. God will only bless you in the direction of your calling. Seeking a blessing in a direction out of your purpose is suicidal. Ask any blessing in the direction of God's purpose for your life and you will certainly have it. There's no limit to which God can bless a man walking into his purpose for living. Begin to seek the right open doors and they shall be opened wide before you. Do not seek another's blessings but seek the God of his blessings.

Nothing is impossible for the man who is in the right direction, on the right path, to the right place of his God ordained destiny. There is no limitation within the sphere of your calling.

2. Your purpose also determines the extent of you revelation.

    God will show you, in fact He can't help but show and tell you, all the things you must know in order to accomplish your vision.

To the prophet Ezekiel the LORD said,

> Son of man, look carefully and listen closely and pay attention to everything I am going to show you, for that is why you have been brought here. Tell the people of Israel everything you see.
> (Ezekiel 40: 4)

He was to look with his eyes

He was to hear with his ears

He was to pay attention to everything he was to be shown.

And he was to tell the house of Israel.

His purpose determined the extent of his revelations. Do not seek to know all that another man knows for you do not have the same calling.

3. Your purpose determines the extent of your anointing.

    Do not seek another man's anointing. God anoints you according to that which He ordained for you to do.

The anointing of Moses was different from that of Joshua.

The anointing of Paul was different from that of Peter.

The anointing of David was different from that of Samuel.

Each one was anointed according to his purpose.

A TEN MINUTES STOP

✤ **Points to Ponder**

a. If you must fulfill your destiny, the presence of God must be your home.

b. Unless a vision is born in God's presence and accomplished first of all in prayer before the Lord, such a vision cannot be realized.

c. God's presence incubates the vision, empowers the vision bearer and propels him into the future.

d. The cross is the centrality of God's will and purpose for mankind.

e. Your destiny determines your blessings and not your blessings determining your destiny.

f. Nothing is impossible for the one who is in the right direction, on the right path, to the right place of his God-ordained destiny.

✤ **Decisions**

....

....

....

....

....

✣ Heartcry

"May Your presence, O Lord, be home for me. Let me dwell in Your secret place, even closer to the cross than ever before. I know nothing is impossible for the one who trusts in You. Therefore, I will put my trust in You alone, to stay in the right direction on the right path to my destiny."

SOME TRUTHS ABOUT A GOD-GIVEN TASK

Let us conclude this book by bringing out some basic truths about every God-given task, with Adam as our case study.

19 Now the Lord God had formed out of the ground all the beasts of the field and all the birds of the air. He brought them to the man to see what he would name them; and whatever the man called each living creature, that was its name. *20* So the man gave names to all the livestock, the birds of the air and all the beasts of the field.
But for Adam no suitable helper was found. *21* So the Lord God caused the man to fall into a deep sleep; and while he was sleeping, he took one of the man's ribs and closed up the place with flesh. *22* Then the Lord God made a woman from the rib he had taken out of the man, and he brought her to the man.

23 The man said,

"This is now bone of my bones
and flesh of my flesh;
she shall be called 'woman,'
for she was taken out of man."
24 For this reason a man will leave his father and mother and be united to his wife, and they will become one flesh.
(Genesis 2:19-24)

We see here that God gave man a task to name the animals, birds and the rest of creation. Man had not been to any school of classification and taxonomy to learn the criteria for naming. All the man had, was his God-given image and likeness and faith that if God could bring the animals for him to name, then he indeed could name them. The Bible says, *"What ever man called… that was its name."*

The task of man was to name. Supposing instead of naming, man spent time asking God for what name to give?

1. When God asks you to do something, the limits within the sphere of your calling are determined by you and not by Him. What ever you decide about it heaven seals it. God's interest was that man should name the animals and so He did not interfere with man's naming. *"What ever the man called… that was its name"*. God did not change any.
2. From the very beginning God gave man the privilege of co-working with Him. He gave man a roll to play in that which would affect his daily life. It is as Adam did his work that God met his needs. To know your needs be engaged in your God-given task.

3. Incomplete tasks were never to be part of man. God made you and gave you the ability to bring to completion that which He gives you.

"So the man gave names to all the livestock"

Failure was never in man's original design. Mediocrity was not in man's original design. When God gives you a task, He sees to it that He endows you with all you need to bring it to completion.

4. God always gives a clearly defined task.
5. The goal of a man cannot be isolated from the rest of his life.
6. Every calling has tasks, which can be evaluated as time passes.
7. Every command of God to a man is tied to his calling.
8. Every need of man is tied to his calling.
9. God meets the needs of the work with what man can offer. This means
    i. God knows your needs: It is the Lord who saw that man had no suitable helper. See Matthew 6:22
    ii. God is able to meet your needs (verse 22): It is God who made the woman without the help or knowledge of man. See Matthew 6:30.

iii. God is willing to meet your needs (verse 22): When God made the woman He brought her to man on His (God's) own volition. See Matthew 6:33.
iv. God only meets your needs with what you can offer Him. You must give out in other to receive. The man had to lose a rib to gain a wife. (verse 21).
v. God's provisions are always compatible with your needs at any given time (verses 23 and 24).

God's Commitment to you

David also said to Solomon his son, "Be strong and courageous, and do the work. Do not be afraid or discouraged, for the Lord God, my God, is with you. He will not fail you or forsake you until all the work for the service of the temple of the Lord is finished."
(1 Chronicles 28:20)

With this in mind, we constantly pray for you, that our God may count you worthy of his calling, and that by his power he may fulfill every good purpose of yours and every act prompted by your faith.
(2 Thessalonicians 1:11)

We said it before, and I now say it again, that all that you need is God's presence and He is committed to be with the person who is doing what He wants him to do, where He wants him to do it and how He wants Him to do it.

From the above verses the following are certain:

1. **God will never fail you:**
   God can never violate His faithfulness, for He cannot deny Himself. It is His very nature to be faithful to His own.

2. **God will not forsake you:**
   He has promised to be with you "even to the end of the age" and He will not abandon you. He will stand with you till your vision is accomplished.

3. **He will keep and protect you from all attacks of the evil one.**
   It is part of the purpose of His presence.

4. **God will fulfill every good purpose of yours.**
   He has already counted you worthy of His calling through the vision He has given you. Now be sure that He is going to fulfill every good purpose of yours as you seek to accomplish your vision.

5. **He will stand with you in every act prompted by your faith.**

More Facts about a God-given Task

1 Listen to me, you islands;
hear this, you distant nations:
Before I was born the Lord called me;
from my birth he has made mention of my name
2 He made my mouth like a sharpened sword,
in the shadow of his hand he hid me;

he made me into a polished arrow
and concealed me in his quiver.
3 He said to me, "You are my servant,
Israel, in whom I will display my splendor."
(Isaiah 49:1-3)

For everybody the Lord calls

1. He equips: "He made my mouth like a sharpened sword".

   God does not only call you but He equips you to be able to fulfil your calling.
2. He protects: *"in the shadow of His hand He hid me"*

   God is committed to protect and defend you to do that which you must do.
3. He molds: *"He made me onto a polished arrow"*

   Not just an arrow with rough edges but a polished arrow! Polishing is a process, which is at times painful. For you to be in His quiver-bank of arrows ready for use. You must be made into a polished arrow. For more on this see my books *"Storms and Flames of Glory"* and *"When all seems fading"*.
4. The only reason for which God calls you or gives you a vision is so that through you God may display His splendor for the islands and distant nations to see. God's vision for you is not for you but for Him and the rest of mankind–the islands and nations.
5. Service for God is never in vain.

You can trust Him; He is your faithful God.
Go therefore and accomplish your vision.
Go therefore and live your life fulfilling your destiny.

A TEN MINUTES STOP

✣ **Points to Meditate on**

a. *Within the sphere of your calling, the limits are determined by you.*

b. *God made you and gave you the ability to bring to completion that which He gives you.*

c. *God meets your needs with what you can offer Him. You must give in order to receive.*

d. *God's purpose for your life is for the benefit of others; drawing mankind closer Him.*

✣ **Decisions**

✣ **Heartcry**

"Lord, You desire for me to accomplish that which is beyond my puny self, touching the lives of others and influencing them God-ward. Thank You for all you've endowed me with. Lord, may I effectively use it for Your glory."

www.ingramcontent.com/pod-product-compliance
Lightning Source LLC
Chambersburg PA
CBHW031244290426
44109CB00012B/434